IMAGINE MOSCOW

ARCHITECTURE PROPAGANDA REVOLUTION

**EDITED BY
ESZTER STEIERHOFFER**

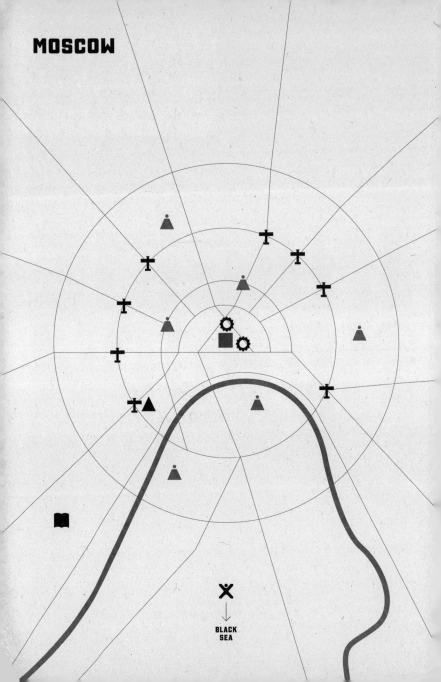

MOSCOW

BLACK
SEA

Introduction:
Imagine Moscow
ESZTER STEIERHOFFER **5**

INTRODUCTION:
IMAGINE MOSCOW
ESZTER STEIERHOFFER

> *Down with the barracks,*
> *cages, apartment kitchens!*
> *Long live communal houses!*
> — N Kuzmin, 1928

I.

The sun rises over the smoky sky and the radio cheerfully greets the morning. It's Moscow, 1 October 1928 — the first day of the first Five-year Plan. The ideal Soviet coal miner's day starts after eight hours of restful sleep, at 6 a.m. sharp. He or she has five minutes for quick exercises before washing his or her face, showering, getting dressed and walking to the communal dining room for the start of the collective breakfast, promptly at 6.25. The Soviet worker has a carefully calculated and perfectly efficient routine to get to the mines, change to a work suit and get the assignment for the eight-hour workday. Work ends at 3 p.m. and a healthy lunch is served in the communal kitchen shortly thereafter at 3.25. Following lunch there's a quiet hour that the comrade can use for rest or self-education. Tea is served at 5.10, followed by four full hours allocated to sport, culture and social activities at the workers' club. Here life dictates its own timetable. Dinner is served at 9.25 and finishes at 9.50, allowing the necessary ten minutes for the comrade to return to the shared dormitories and get ready to sleep. At 10 p.m. the lights go out.[1]

As the architect Nikolay Kuzmin further explains in his experimental proposal for ideal Soviet life: unmarried adults sleep by gender in rooms for six, while couples are assigned adjacent rooms connected by a door that can be shut in case of divorce. Children, organized in age groups, sleep in large shared rooms. These bedrooms are intended for sleep only, while life is lived collectively in the shared social spaces: the dining room and the workers' club. Food is distributed through a central mechanized system.

Children under fifteen are fed separately, and follow a special diet. Traditional family life is abolished in the house communes, and children live apart from their parents. Women work either in the mine or in the collective servicing of the commune — all women are independent and employed. Pregnant women are transferred to special units, and their daily timetable is adjusted on the basis of medical advice. Recent mothers remain in designated living spaces for a short while. Advanced technology

Arkady Shaikhet, *Steelworks*, 1935

facilitates modern, collective living of the highest efficiency. The communal house is strictly organized around the worker's daily routine and needs. Such organization not only accommodates but further contributes to the systematic cultural development of the socialist individual.[2]

Is it possible to imagine everyday life so minutely organized? While it remains a thought-experiment, Kuzmin's proposal for the fundamental restructuring of the everyday reveals the depth of revolutionary thinking — the basis of revolutionary architecture.

II.

Moscow, the industrial centre of Russia, with the largest working-class population, was chosen as the new capital of the Bolshevik state a year after the October Revolution, in 1918. And with that move, the old imperial city swiftly began to seem inadequate to the new vision of society that the revolution promised. As housing across the city was appropriated and redistributed, a new idea emerged: communal living. The first architectural representation of a 'house commune' was shown at an exhibition organized by the Narkompros (People's Commissariat for Education) in 1920, where Nikolay Ladovsky's experimental drawings of the Communal House gained instant fame.[3] The spatial organization of his multi-storey building implied a whole new model of social interaction. It was arranged in a spiral, which was intended to coalesce the residents into a greater collective unity. While the spiral of Ladovsky's plan — as in Tatlin's design for the Third International — remained a symbol, the 1920s saw more utilitarian experimentations that explored the architectural foundations of a new life in the post-revolutionary cities of the Soviet Union. Dreaming up whole new typologies of housing, architects such as Kuzmin and Moisei Ginzburg relied on precise socio-economic evaluations of the Soviet worker's ideal daily routine. Their functionalist approach to life proposed a new image for architecture as much as a new model for the organization of society.

Feverish contemporary debates about the development of the Soviet economy and the improvement of workers' living conditions were closely tied with the issue of emancipation and employment of women. In 1918, the first Soviet Constitution declared the equal rights of men and women. Radical proposals for the 'communal house' challenged the most fundamental social unit: the family. In his 1928 study of the new social and architectural model that the communal house represented, Kuzmin declared: 'The proletariat must destroy the family as a prime device of oppression and exploitation.'[4] The traditional division of labour was to be replaced by a new system in which the 'communal nursery' and the 'kitchen factory' allowed for the woman's liberation and her participation in work and public life as equal to men. Beside the house communes, trade unions commissioned the nationwide construction of new, dedicated buildings for workers' clubs. Physical exercise, ideological education and active social participation were seen as the basic ingredients of the ideal life in a new egalitarian society.

The heroic role assigned to architecture was no less than to create the blueprint of society. Kuzmin's daily routine for the communal house remained a fantasy, eerily reminiscent of Yevgeny Zamyatin's 1921 dystopian novel *We*, where citizens reduced to numbers lived their life in full public view and followed a routine dictated by the 'Table of Hours'. But housing was only one aspect of the city that was deemed ripe for reinvention. A new generation of Soviet architects set about creating new monuments and new institutions. In a climate where, briefly, anything seemed possible, their dream-like projects willed an alternative reality for countless sites around the city. Even the very idea of 'the city' was hotly contested. Debates unfolded between keen supporters of urbanization and those who dismissed the urban form as sheer capitalist expression.

In his *Man with a Movie Camera*, also known as *Living Russia*, Dziga Vertov portrayed the new life of citizens at work and play in the speeding city.[5] His experimental silent film — shot in the four major Soviet cities of Kiev, Kharkov, Moscow and Odessa — became the cornerstone of the emerging medium of cinema, Lenin's favoured new art form. Vertov's cutting-edge cinematic techniques such as slow motion, montage and jump cuts allowed for a new way of seeing and experiencing the urban image, transforming urban reality into a new visionary landscape.

This impulse to meld the old city with the new was also a central principle of Alexey Shchusev's 1924 general plan of Moscow, which proposed to introduce new infrastructure — such as the metro or new spacious boulevards animated by modern architecture — while preserving the functional and culturally significant fabric of the old city. Though Shchusev's plan was dismissed by the Communist Party for its overly preservationist approach, it influenced a generation of designers and urban planners. Between 1919 and 1920 Alexander Rodchenko designed a series of architectural compositions in which he replaced the skyline of old Moscow with a new parallel facade suspended above the city. Similarly, El Lissitzky's so-called 'Cloud Iron' proposed a new type of horizontal skyscraper that appeared to hover several

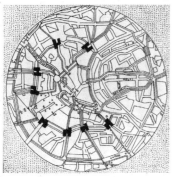

El Lissitzky, *Plan of the Centre of Moscow with Skyscrapers in Ring A*, 1923-5

storeys above street level.[6] His urban plan consisted of a ring of eight glass towers, strategically placed at the intersections of the inner boulevard circle and its main arteries. A whole new aesthetic for the city of the future, it also offered a functional solution to the problem of overcrowding and the lack of public transport in Moscow, linking the office and living space of the upper floors directly with new tram and metro stations below. Just as illusory, but far less rational, were Georgy Krutikov and Ladovsky's plans for the *Flying City* in 1928, which addressed the problems of urban overcrowding by proposing a dream-like fleet of aerial buildings floating above ground and colonizing the sky.

In June 1925, the year of the public announcement of his 'Cloud Iron' proposal, Lissitzky wrote to his wife: 'The position is this: the ecstatic period of the Revolution is over. Now it's the working day — but art is holiday. And we want art back, *the new art of architecture*.'[7] Architecture's new task in redefining the urban landscape implied the reinvention of

VKhUTEMAS architecture students with three-dimensional models, 1920s

architecture itself: its techniques, materials and languages, often in close dialogue with the avant-garde movements in art. One important vehicle for this reinvention was the VKhUTEMAS, the Higher Art and Technical Studios of Moscow. Established in 1920, it soon became a leading centre of spatial experimentation for Constructivism, Suprematism and Rationalism across the fields of art, architecture and the applied arts. Teachers and their students set out to advance a new revolutionary language for architecture and the city. Among them, Yakov Chernikhov spent a lifetime developing his new alphabet for modern architecture through his series of books: *Fundamentals of Contemporary Architecture* (1930), *The Construction of Architectural and Machine Forms* (1931), and his *101 Architectural fantasies* (1933). While none of these designs was meant to go beyond painterly experiments with form and language, in retrospect, Chernikhov's industrial capriccios became a surprisingly accurate echo of our current landscape.

At the Vitebsk Art School, Ilya Chashnik and El Lissitzky, close collaborators of Kazimir Malevich, developed his Suprematist ideas of the fourth dimension — implying a sensation of levitation that allowed the viewer to attain a higher level of consciousness — in the field of architecture. While Chashnik's abstract spatial explorations remained on paper, Lissitzky moved from the space of the canvas to that of the city. His theory of the PROUN (an acronym standing for the Russian phrase 'project for the affirmation of the new') inserted abstract forms of Suprematist compositions first into the space of a room and later into the space of the city. Lissitzky, like other Suprematists, compared the transformative power of revolution in society to that of the insertion of abstract art into the lived environment.

The Suprematist and Constructivist revolution — the radical transformation of the city — remained largely on paper, at first for economic reasons, and later for ideological or technological ones. A less monumental but nonetheless potent transformation happened on the scale of domestic objects. Malevich, Suetin and Chashnik saw their work realized by porcelain and textile factories, as did many of their contemporaries.

Ilya Chashnik, *Suprematist Ornament*, 1927-8

Lissitzky, Rodchenko and fellow artists Lyubov Popova, Gustav Klutsis and Valentina Kulagina transformed the culture of printed media through magazines, posters and other state propaganda. The Russian folk tradition, a romanticized view of the past, was soon replaced by a new Soviet vernacular built on images of a seemingly imminent future. These images — in stark contrast with the reality of a city still in its feudalist form, inhabited by a starving population — colonized people's imaginations and the stuff of everyday life. On cinema screens, on the pages of books and magazines, on advertising boards, in temporary street decorations, on tableware and domestic textiles, a parallel, imaginary Moscow unfolded.

This new Moscow was to become the centre of a socialist world of cosmic dimensions. As Shchusev remarked at the First Congress of Soviet Architects: 'We are the only direct successors of Rome; only in socialist society and with socialist technology is the construction of even greater dimensions and greater artistic perfection possible.'[8] In pursuit of these greater dimensions, Russian artists and intellectuals looked both to the future and to the past. In *Aelita*, the first Soviet sci-fi film, based on Aleksey Tolstoy's 1923 novel, the Queen of Mars falls in love with a Soviet engineer who colonized the planet and reformed Martian society to the Soviet model. Meanwhile, Ivan Leonidov's series of mesmerizing architectural fantasies *The City of the Sun* interpreted Moscow as a socialist version of Tommaso Campanella's sixteenth-century book of the same name — the centre of a global egalitarian society where knowledge is a substitute for religion, reason takes over from superstition and libraries

ESZTER STEIERHOFFER

replace the churches of the Tsarist era. The shrines of this new society were no longer erected to the gods, but to the new leaders of socialism. Lenin's body was preserved in the glass sarcophagus designed by Melnikov in the belief that science could one day restore the leader to life on earth.[9] Zamyatin rightly reminds us of this paradox: 'knowledge, absolutely sure of its infallibility, is faith'.[10]

By the mid-1930s, the image of the Communal House was supplanted by that of the Palace of the Soviets. This monumental assembly building marked the end of the revolutionary language of the avant-garde and the arrival of a more conservative language of officialdom, one that favoured neoclassical facades and Socialist Realist imagery.[11] In 1935, following the bitter history of so many rejected Constructivist plans, Moscow's first metro line was finally completed. The stations' architecture oozed classical grandeur, their luxurious marble halls offering the opulence of Versailles for the enjoyment of the proletariat. This nostalgic reversal in style signalled a shift in the dialogue between the real and the projected image of architecture. If the unbuilt landscape of the early post-revolutionary years aimed to influence and reinvent the realm of the real, by the time Stalin gained full power, it was the proletariat's imagination that the architecture of a new Soviet realism leveraged. Architecture gained new life as full-blown propaganda: its representative image became more important than its function.

The Palace of the Soviets was intended to exemplify Stalin's vision of an all-powerful state.[12] It was to be the tallest building in the world, taller than the Empire State Building in New York, which was completed the year that Stalin's competition was announced, in 1931 — a year that also saw the beginnings of one of the greatest famines in the history of the Soviet Union. Significantly, it replaced the largest Tsarist cathedral, in the heart of Moscow, with a monument dedicated to the Soviet Union and its immortal leader, Lenin[13]. Boris Iofan's winning competition entry soon became one of the most circulated images of Soviet times — gracing magazine covers, festive street decorations, hand-painted lacquer boxes, porcelain plates and vases, woven and lace curtains as well as futuristic animations and photomontages. The Palace remained a recurring motif across the country for decades after it was aborted in the early stages of construction. It was to become the ultimate architectural phantom of the Soviet capital.

LEFT Boris Iofan, Vladimir Gelfreikh and Vladimir Shchuko, the model of the *Palace of the Soviets* as exhibited at the Paris World's exposition, 1937 RIGHT *The Empire State Building* featured in the film *King Kong*, 1933

The Palace was crowned with a one-hundred-metre-tall statue of Lenin more than three times the size of the Statue of Liberty. Facing the Kremlin, its giant finger would point at the Mausoleum in Red Square where the leader's embalmed body remains to this day on public display. The Lenin Mausoleum — the geographical centre of Moscow and the spiritual centre of the Soviet Union — captivated the imagination of Soviet society. Artists and architects as well as laymen, factory workers, peasants and students competed to design the mausoleum and to create a new iconography for the personal cult of Lenin which found its ultimate expression in the building of the Palace of the Soviets. The final and greatest of the monuments dedicated to Lenin's cult was, however, never completed. The monumental construction came to a halt with the German invasion of the Soviet Union in 1941. Its significant site — first converted into an open-air swimming pool and then, in the post-Soviet era, restored to its Tsarist glory with an exact replica of the original Cathedral of Christ the Saviour — stands as a reminder of a turbulent succession of regimes and ideologies. Again, Zamyatin's words reverberate: 'There is no final one; revolutions are infinite.'

III.

The Russian October Revolution and its cultural aftermath represented a heroic moment in design history. Its visionary images and ideas are still reflected in the work of contemporary architects and designers. The exhibition *Imagine Moscow* explores what remained of the largely imaginary landscapes and phantoms of an idealized Soviet capital as proposed by a bold generation of architects. It presents six unbuilt architectural case studies that were meant to be sited in and around Moscow. The seventh case study is the Lenin Mausoleum, located at the city's geographical and ideological centre. Each offers unique insight into the culture of the time and introduces a theme central to Soviet life and ideology: communal ways of living, democratization of health, work and female emancipation, knowledge sharing, globalization, propaganda and mass communication.

This cast of 'phantoms', architectural monuments of the vanished world of the Soviet Union, survive despite never being realized. Their architectural visions were first rediscovered by the 'paper architects' of the 1970s and their echoes, ever since, resound. The neo-avant-garde generation and their nostalgic thirst for a long-lost future became obsessed with the inherent utopian paradox of early Soviet architecture. Taking a different path, the ultimate aim of the exhibition, as of this publication, is to revisit their original visions in the present time, and to ask again the radical — if often unanswered — questions posed by the Russian avant-garde, which remain highly relevant to contemporary life. In this same spirit, the exhibition assumes an attitude, inspired by the spatial experiments of Tatlin or Lissitzky, which prefers communication and engagement with its subjects to more traditional ways of framing or historicizing objects.

The presentation of the six architectural case studies became the fundamental challenge — as well as the main inspiration — for the exhibition's design. As the drawings could not be transported from Moscow to London, the architectural 'phantoms' of the post-revolutionary city remained phantoms also within the show. This invited unconventional methods of presentation that reactivate the material through contemporary design. Kuehn Malvezzi's exhibition design is arranged in a spiral which connects the plans, models, reproductions and projections of the six unrealized projects. Beyond its conceptual resonance

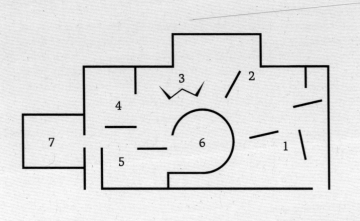

Kuehn Malvezzi Architects, *Imagine Moscow: Architecture, Propaganda, Revolution* exhibition plan, 2017: (1) Cloud Iron: *Colonizing the sky* (2) Lenin Institute: *Educating the new man* (3) Health Factory: *The body as machine* (4) Communal House: *Emancipating women* (5) Commissariat of Heavy Industry: *Industry is the new landscape* (6) Palace of the Soviets: *The eternal monument* (7) Lenin Mausoleum: *Cult of the leader*

with avant-garde architecture, this spatial arrangement became instrumental in conveying the evolution of early Soviet design as well as juxtaposing the early experimental language with later Stalinist state propaganda. The exhibition's innovative spatial design is complemented by the environmental graphics of Kellenberger-White, which evoke the fragments of an imaginary city in a suggestive size.

Original objects of art and design, the remarkable traces of a post-revolutionary Moscow as imagined by its inhabitants, contextualize the architectural projects within the show. From Suprematist tableware to Constructivist magazines, propaganda posters, textile design, photomontage, film and newsreels manifest the dreams and aspirations of a generation of artists and architects and present an archaeology of a future that could never be realized. The first part of this publication, a sequence of seven carefully edited visual essays, catalogues this diverse material, which is organized around the six architectural case studies

and their imaginary epicentre, the Lenin Mausoleum. The second part, three essays and the historical chronology, contextualize and explore the themes evoked by the case studies through further reading.
Richard Anderson's essay 'The Spectacle of Socialist Moscow' reviews the different urban models proposed for post-revolutionary Moscow and the ideas that these urban images mediate. In 'Lissitzky's "Amerikanizm"', Jean-Louis Cohen introduces a text by El Lissitzky and explores the transfer of architectural concepts across the globe. Written in 1925, '"Amerikanizm" in European Architecture' sets out the architect's new typology for a skyscraper. Finally, as the Russian avant-garde comes to a close with the Palace of the Soviets, this case study is placed last in the exhibition and this publication. 'The Socialist Vatican' by Deyan Sudjic narrates the curious history of this contested and highly symbolic site, starting from its early days until the present.

This book and exhibition can only offer a glance into the immensely rich and diverse material hidden in Moscow's archives and private collections — the starting point of this precarious curatorial adventure. Our endeavour, by bringing together lesser-known architectural projects with iconic works of the avant-garde and pieces of overt propaganda, was to create a more nuanced perspective on this controversial historical period. The curatorial project was twofold: it has aimed to reinforce overlooked links between works and overarching ideas as well as to underline the importance of architectural thinking in early Soviet culture. It is hoped that this publication will prompt further investigations into the field and into the archives of Moscow, where other histories remain to be discovered.

1   The timetable for the ideal day of the coal miner was calculated by architect Nikolay Kuzmin and first published in *CA* magazine. See Nikolay Kuzmin, 'The Problem of Scientific Organisation of Life' in *CA* 1930, no. 3, 14 – 17.

2   Kuzmin, ibid, 15

3   XIX Vystavka VTsVB Otdela IZO Narkomprosa ['19th State Exhibition'] in Moscow, Summer-Autumn 1920. The twenty-two participants also included Alexander Rodchenko, Georgy Mapu, Varvara Stepanova, Vladimir Krinsky and Wassily Kandinsky.

4   Kuzmin, 'O rabochem zhilischnom stroitelstve', [On the building of worker's dwellings] in *CA* 1928, no. 3, 83.

5   Dziga Vertov's film dates to 1929.

6   Lissitzky referred to his horizontal skyscrapers as '*Wolkenbügel*', a German term that literally translates as 'hanger for clouds'. In the late nineteenth century, before the term 'skyscraper' became widely used, 'cloud-presser' was the most popular term in the European context to describe these new architectural structures. Lissitzky's design is most often referred to in English as 'Cloud Iron'.

7   Sophie Lissitzky-Küppers, *El Lissitzky: Life, Letters, Texts*, intro. Herbert Read (London: Thames and Hudson, 1968), 65.

8   The First Congress of Soviet Architects was organized in 1937 in Moscow. See *Russian State Archive of Literature and Art* (RGALI), fund No 674, inv., archival unit 43.

9   See John Gray, *The Immortalization Commission: The Strange Quest to Cheat Death* (London: Allen Lane, 2011).

10 Yevgeny Zamyatin, *We* (New York: Avon books, 1987) translated by Mirra Ginzburg, p.59.

11 While the term 'Socialist Realism' first appeared in 1932, it was adopted as official artistic doctrine in 1934 at the First All-Union Congress of Soviet Writers.

12 The four main stages of the competition for the Palace of the Soviets took place between 1931-3. Boris Iofan finalized his winning entry with architects Vladimir Shchuko and Vladimir Gelfreikh in the following four years.

13 The Cathedral of Christ the Saviour was consecrated during the coronation of Tsar Alexander III in 1883; at the time, it was the largest cathedral in Russia. This tsarist symbol was demolished in 1931 in order to make way for the Palace of the Soviets.

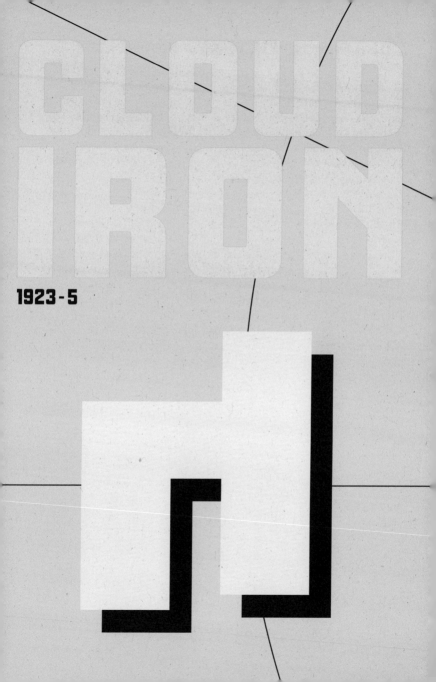

COLONIZING THE SKY

El Lissitzky's speculative plan for rebuilding Moscow was based on inventing a new building type, the so-called 'Cloud Iron', a horizontal skyscraper. He envisaged a network of these structures around Moscow's Boulevard Ring. The eight buildings were to be placed at major intersections, directly connecting offices and living space on the upper floors to the new tram and metro stations at street level. Lissitzky's idea of maximizing the horizontal surface of his skyscrapers meant to address, in one gesture, Moscow's pressing problems of overcrowding and inadequate public transport.

While there was a practical justification for the plan, El Lissitzky was also moved by the ambition of giving Moscow a new skyline to replace its feudal past. Like many of his contemporaries, he believed that the insertion of Suprematist and Constructivist forms into the everyday environment symbolized the transformative power of revolution in society. He called his experimental compositions the 'communist foundation of steel and concrete for the people of the earth'.

While his skyscrapers remained unbuilt, colonizing the sky became an obsession, with aviation motifs featuring prominently in the art and propaganda of the Soviet Union.

El Lissitzky, *Design for the Cloud Iron*, views from the Kremlin, 1925

El Lissitzky, *Proun 1E* (*The City*), 1919-21

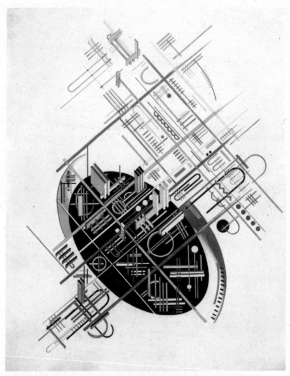

Yakov Chernikhov, *101 Architectural Fantasies, composition no. 57,* 1933

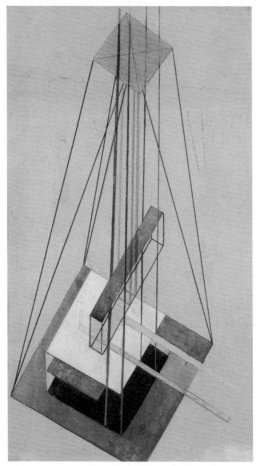

Gustav Klutsis, *Architectural Study*, 1921-2

Innokenty Kychakov, *Festival Design, Central Park for Culture and Recovery* (*Gorky Park*), 1929

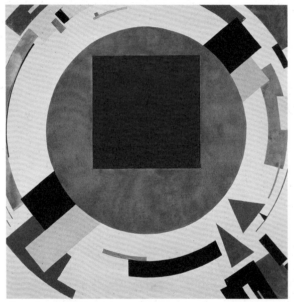

El Lissitzky, *Proun*, 1922-3

CLOUD IRON

Lyubov Popova, *Suprematist Composition*, 1917

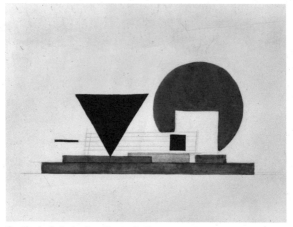

Ilya Chashnik, *Project for a Suprematist Monument*, 1927

CLOUD IRON

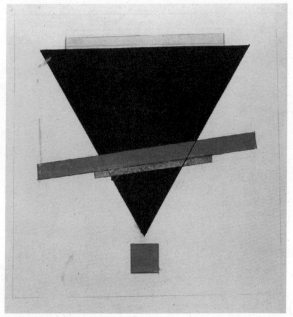

Ilya Chashnik, *Red Square UNOVIS*, 1924

Nikolai Suetin, *Sketch for a Chair*, 1927

CLOUD IRON

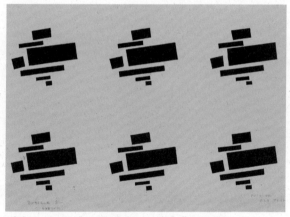

Nikolai Suetin, *Suprematist Surface Forms*, textile design, c 1921

Pesochenskaya Pottery Factory, 'And our ultimatum', 1929

Valentina Kulagina, 'To the defence of the USSR', 1931

Maria Bri-Bein, 'Woman proletarian, seize aircraft, go to schools and colleges of civil aviation!', 1931

FROM DARKNESS TO LIGHT, FROM BATTLE TO BOOK, FROM MISERY TO HAPPINESS

|

NIKOLAY KOGOUT
1921

LENIN INSTITUTE

1927

EDUCATING THE NEW MAN

Ivan Leonidov's Lenin Institute was designed to be 'the collective knowledge centre of the USSR'. The monumental central library was intended to congregate all human knowledge. It would have accommodated fifteen million books in five generously proportioned reading rooms alongside a planetarium, auditorium and a number of scientific lecture theatres that connected to the entire world by a powerful wireless transmitter.

Lenin set out to reconfigure Moscow's iconography to reflect a new political idea. Fighting illiteracy and educating the new Soviet man and woman were central to Soviet political propaganda. One important influence on Soviet intellectuals and architects was the sixteenth-century priest Tommaso Campanella's vision of an egalitarian utopia. His book *The City of the Sun* described a community in which architecture was used to convey the old principles on which it was founded. Campanella's vision resonated with the Bolshevik goal to replace religion with a new doctrine of scientific reason.

Leonidov's proposals for the ideal city elevated the worldwide proletariat to cosmic dimensions in which the personal cult of Lenin was comparable to the pagan cult of the Sun. In *Aelita*, the first ever Soviet sci-fi film, a despotic society on Mars was reformed to the model of the Soviet Union, and the hero figure was a studious engineer.

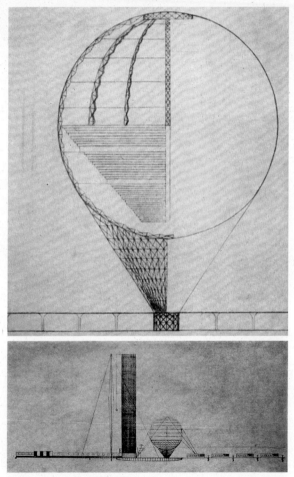

Ivan Leonidov, *Lenin Institute*, 1927

Ivan Leonidov, *United Nations Building*, 1947-8

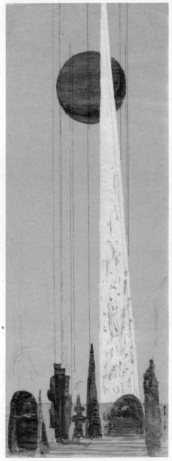

Ivan Leonidov, *The City of the Sun, Distant View*,
1943-59

Ivan Leonidov, *The City of the Sun*, 1957-8

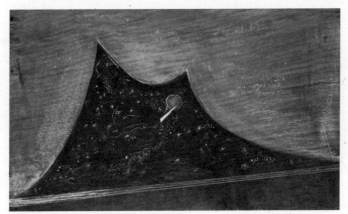

Ivan Leonidov, *Monument to the First Sputnik*, 1958

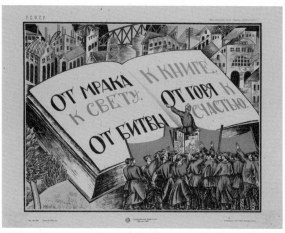

Nikolay Kogout, 'From darkness to light, from battle to book, from misery to happiness', 1921

Unknown, 'Worldwide Peoples' Armed Forces', 1919

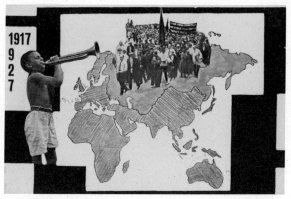

Karel Teige, *1917-1927*, 1927

Boris Efimov, *Our Rise ... And Their Landing*, 1933

Alexander Rodchenko, *Circus-Acrobats*, 1938

THERE IS NO MORE BEAUTIFUL CLOTHING IN THE WORLD, THAN THE BRONZE OF MUSCLES AND FRESHNESS OF SKIN

|

VLADIMIR MAYAKOVSKY
1927

HEALTH FACTORY

1928 - 9

THE BODY AS MACHINE

Nikolay Sokolov's highly expressive graphic plan for the Health Factory proposed a retreat for tired Muscovites in the Matsesta district on the coast of the Black Sea. Like other Constructivists, Sokolov was interested in the idea of the 'living cell'. The project consisted of individual capsules for isolated rest and a communal hall for eating and other collective activities. The common areas were designed to be efficient and mechanized, with conveyor belts to distribute food in order to prevent the queues that resulted from a conventional waiting system.

Sokolov's proposal promoted productive rest as a key element in the new Soviet society. The idea of the holiday was presented as a means of restoring the productive capacities of the workers. As the USSR Conference on Workers' Vacations declared: 'Like a machine, a person needs repair and recuperation: socialist leisure restores the proletarian machine-body.'

A vacation was to be a relaxing experience but also an edifying one. To this end, health factories combined recreation, games, sports and other regulated activities different from the worker's ordinary daily routine. Throughout the Soviet period, physical fitness was a national priority, and daily exercise was promoted by vigorous public health campaigns.

Nikolay Sokolov, *Hotel Resort,
Individual House*, 1928

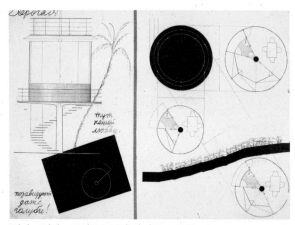

Nikolay Sokolov, *Hotel Resort, Individual House*, 1928

HEALTH FACTORY

Nikolay Sokolov, *Hotel Resort, Social Complex*, 1928

El Lissitzky, design for magazine cover, 1922

Platon Ippolitov, 'Free aerobics', 1933

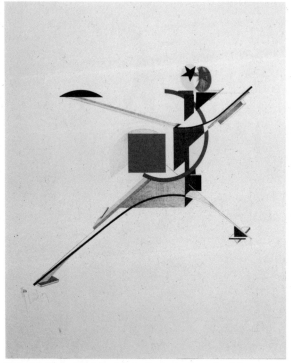

El Lissitzky, three-dimensional design for the electro-mechanical opera, *Victory Over the Sun, The New Man,* 1923

Rajnis, *Untitled*, 1926

OPPOSITE Ivanovo-Voznesensk Factories, textile fragment, 1928-32

Vera Gitsevich, *For the Proletarian Park of Culture and Leisure*, 1930s

THE PROLETARIAT MUST DESTROY THE FAMILY AS A PRIME DEVICE OF OPPRESSION AND EXPLOITATION

|

NIKOLAY KUZMIN
1928

COMMUNAL HOUSE

1919-20

EMANCIPATING WOMEN

Nikolay Ladovsky was one of the first architects to address the idea of communal living, a key concept of the Soviet regime that was intended to revolutionize society by destroying the traditional family structure and transforming the role of women. Utilizing the spatial diagram of the spiral, Ladovsky's experimental design for the Communal House merged individual living units into a single space. Like Tatlin's famous *Monument to the Third International*, the project's highly symbolic form was to be understood as an allusion to progress in time and society.

The lack of public housing and inadequacy of the old buildings prompted a whole new generation of Soviet architects to experiment with ideas of communal living. In collaboration with social scientists, they designed housing programmes and related communal facilities with the aim of shaping and controlling socialist life.

Communal kitchens and nurseries were introduced so that women could dedicate their free time to self-improvement. The emancipation of women was ultimately aimed at adding women to the workplace, one of the cornerstones of the new economic model of the Soviet Union. However, the abolition of the family structure, with children raised communally, remained unachieved.

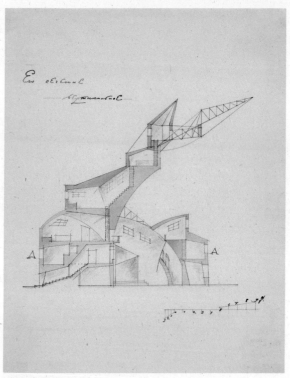

Nikolay Ladovsky, *Communal House*, 1919

Georgy Mapu, *Communal House*, 1919-20

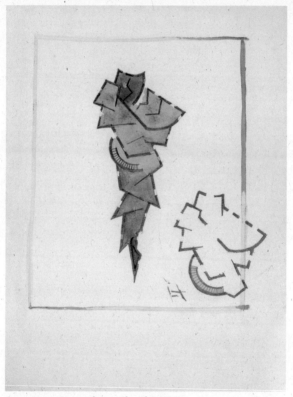

Georgy Mapu, *Communal House, Floor Plan*, 1920

Georgy Mapu, *Communal House*, 1919-20

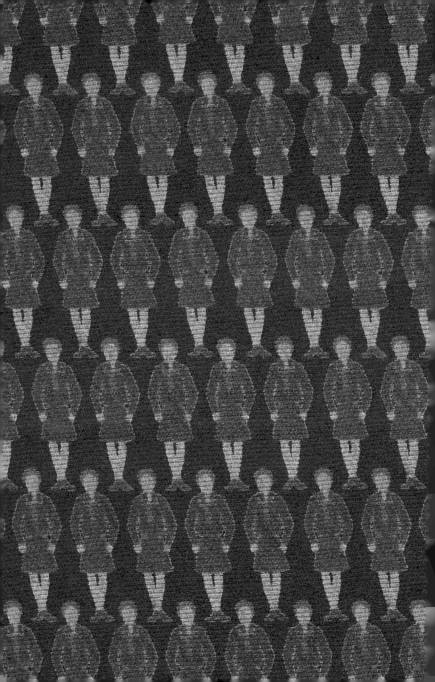

Unknown, 'By organizing day nurseries, playgrounds, kitchen factories, canteens and mechanical laundries, we will get 1,600,000 new working women', 1931

Valentina Kulagina, *The International Day of Working Women*, 1930

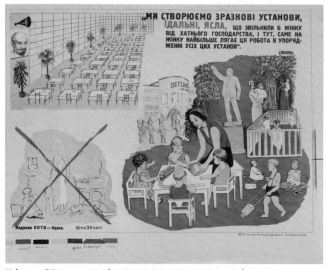

Unknown, 'We create exemplary institutions, canteens, nurseries', 1930s

Valentina Kulagina, *Krasnaya Niva N. 12*, 1930

WE GROW OUT OF IRON

|

ALEXEY GASTEV
1923

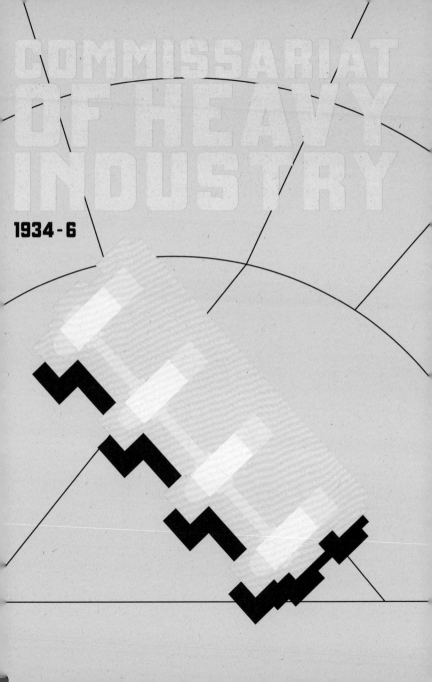

COMMISSARIAT OF HEAVY INDUSTRY

1934 - 6

INDUSTRY IS THE NEW LANDSCAPE

The monumental government building of the Commissariat of Heavy Industry would have occupied a site of just under ten acres directly opposite the Lenin Mausoleum on Red Square. As part of Stalin's Greater Plan for Moscow, it would have required the demolition of a significant proportion of Moscow's old town. One of the largest of its kind, the two-stage design competition received more than a hundred entries from Soviet architects.

While no winning design was selected, the entries include outstanding examples of a new type of representative architecture. Konstantin Melnikov's proposal set out to symbolize the achievements of Soviet industry. Its two forty-storey buildings, connected by an external escalator, were to be embellished with monumental sculptures representing the First and Second Five-year Plans. The Vesnin brothers accommodated the brief in four towers that were to mirror the towers within the walls of the Kremlin.

The large-scale competition for the Commissariat building underlined the importance of industry in building socialism. The rapid industrialization captivated the imagination of many architects of the time. Among these, Yakov Chernikhov's playful architectural fantasies developed a new language for an industrial landscape, which would become the backdrop of the new life in the Soviet Union.

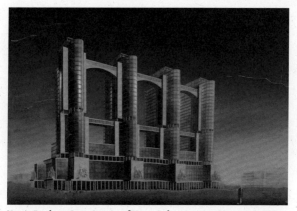

Vesnin Brothers, Commissariat of Heavy Industry competition entry, 1934

Ivan Leonidov, Commissariat of Heavy Industry competition entry, 1934

Konstantin Melnikov, Commissariat of Heavy Industry competition entry, 1934

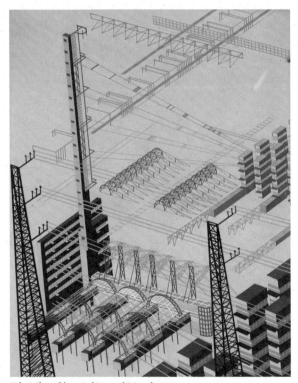

Yakov Chernikhov, *Architectural Fairytale*, 1933

Gustav Klutsis, *Lenin in a Factory,* c 1929

Arkady Shaikhet, *Assembling at a Metal Plant*, 1930s

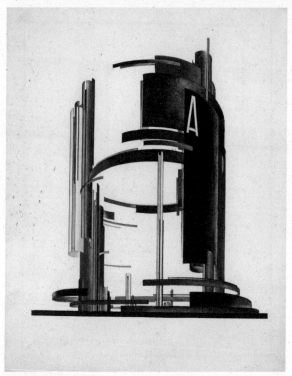

Yakov Chernikhov, *Architectural Fairytale*, late 1920s

Valentina Kulagina, 'We build', c 1930

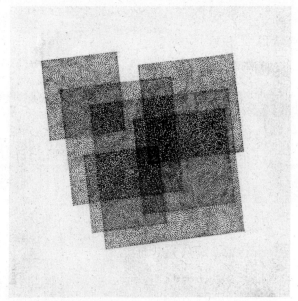

Yakov Chernikhov, *Untitled*, 1920

Gustav Klutsis, *Untitled*, 1930

'WE'
COMES
FROM
GOD
'I'
FROM
THE
DEVIL

|

YEVGENY ZAMYATIN
1922

PALACE OF THE SOVIETS

1931-41

THE ETERNAL MONUMENT

The Palace of the Soviets was conceived as the single most dramatic expression of Soviet power. Designed to accommodate Party Assemblies and mass gatherings, it would have been the tallest building in the world. It was designed for one of Moscow's most prominent sites, once occupied by the Cathedral of Christ the Saviour, the city's largest church which had been dynamited by Stalin.

The competition for the Palace of the Soviets took place in four stages between 1931 and 1933. Boris Iofan's winning project was chosen personally by Stalin for its monumentality. His plan was then developed until 1937 with the collaboration of Vladimir Shchuko and Vladimir Gelfreikh. Marking the demise of Soviet architecture's avant-garde phase, Iofan's project was propaganda in built form.

With a height of 416 metres and topped with a 100-metre statue of Lenin, the building was designed to be taller than the Empire State Building in New York. Construction started in 1937 but was terminated by the German invasion in 1941. After the war, Stalin's successor, Nikita Khrushchev, had its foundations turned into an outdoor swimming pool. This too disappeared in 1994 to make way for the replica of the original cathedral that now stands on the site.

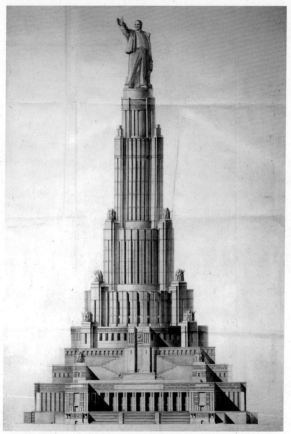

Boris Iofan, Vladimir Gelfreikh and Vladimir Shchuko, *The Palace of the Soviets*, c 1937

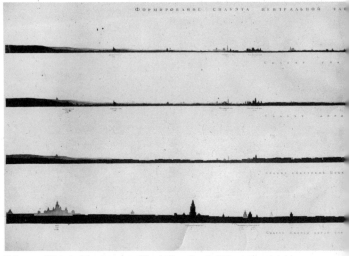

Unknown, 'Historical development of the skyline of central Moscow', undated

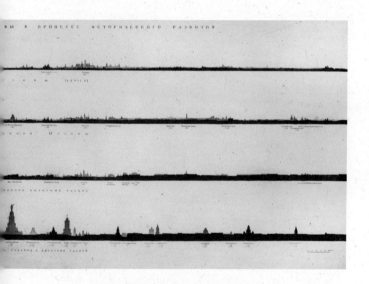

Boris Iofan, *The Palace of the Soviets*, view of the interior, 1944

Boris Iofan, Vladimir Gelfreikh and Vladimir Shchuko, *The Palace of the Soviets, Final Version*, 1937

Boris Iofan, *The Palace of the Soviets,* c 1933

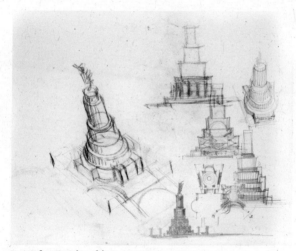

Boris Iofan, *The Palace of the Soviets*, 1933-7

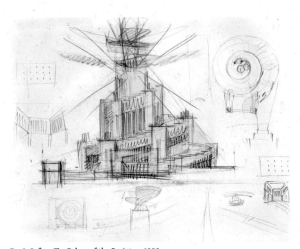

Boris Iofan, *The Palace of the Soviets*, c 1933

Gustav Klutsis, *Untitled*, 1929

Gustav Klutsis, *Untitled*, 1930

PALACE OF THE SOVIETS

LENIN
MAUSOLEUM
1924-30

CULT OF THE LEADER

When Lenin died in 1924 Mayakovsky wrote: 'Lenin, even now, is more alive than the living.' The atheist leader of the Communist revolution became the object of a carefully orchestrated cult that took on an increasingly overt religious significance in its iconography.

Lenin was buried in Red Square, just outside the Kremlin, on three separate occasions. The first was in a temporary wooden mausoleum designed by Alexey Shchusev, which was built in less than a week. By the summer of 1924, Shchusev had drawn up plans for a more permanent wooden structure. But soon after it was built, a national competition for the design of a permanent mausoleum was announced. Numerous entries from professional architects as well as workers, clerks, teachers and pupils were received. However, again, it was Shchusev's design that was chosen to be realized.

The building was completed in 1930 and still stands on Red Square. Lenin's embalmed body lies in a glass sarcophagus designed by Melnikov and placed in the centre of a cube-shaped Memorial Hall with a stepped ceiling. The Mausoleum became the epicentre of the Soviet Union, Lenin's monumental index finger was supposed to point it out from atop the Palace of the Soviets.

Alexey Shchusev, *Lenin Mausoleum,* 1924

Gustav Klutsis, *Monument to our Fallen Leaders*, 1924

Gustav Klutsis, *Monument to our Fallen Leaders*, 1924

LENIN, EVEN NOW, IS MORE ALIVE THAN THE LIVING

|

VLADIMIR MAYAKOVSKY
1924

Unknown, 'Lenin's city is the city of universal literacy', 1931

Georgy Kibardin, 'We will build Lenin's squadron of airships', 1931

Mikhail Balyasny, 'We will make the USSR the country of socialist industry and electrification', 1930

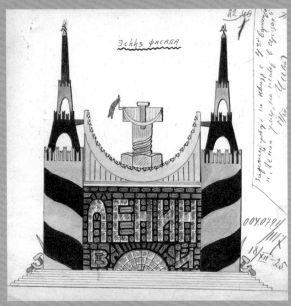

P Ustinov, Competition entry for the Lenin Mausoleum in Moscow, 1924

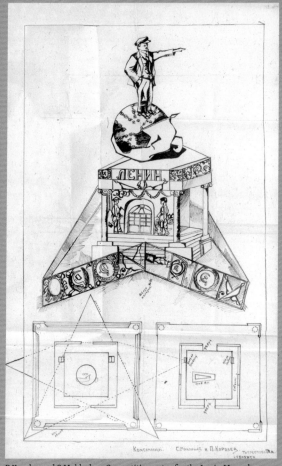

P Korolev and S Maklashev, Competition entry for the Lenin Mausoleum in Moscow, 1924

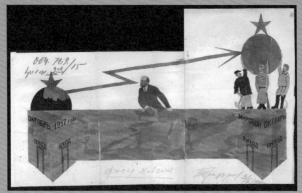

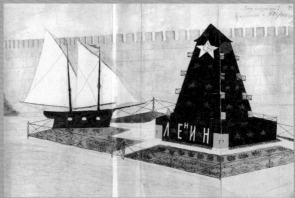

ABOVE B Prokhorov, Competition entry for the Lenin Mausoleum in Moscow, 1924
BELOW A Smirnov, Competition entry for the Lenin Mausoleum in Moscow, 1924

N Ryabov, Competition entry for the Lenin Mausoleum in Moscow, 1924

P Berkutov, Competition entry for the Lenin Mausoleum in Moscow, 1924

THE SPECTACLE OF SOCIALIST MOSCOW

RICHARD ANDERSON

Readers of *USSR in Construction*, the Soviet Union's multilingual propaganda magazine, found a striking image of Moscow on the first page of the September 1931 issue. Showing not the historic centre, but rather a recently constructed housing district, the image underlined the tensions between the old and the new. Low, single-storey barracks and construction yards occupy the foreground. At the centre is the Usacheva Street Housing development, designed by A Meshkov and others and built between 1925 and 1928. The towers of Novodevichii Monastery are visible at the upper left, while an expanse of open land extends deep into the background of the image. Lenin's shadow, inserted in the darkroom, looms over the scene, his finger pointing to Moscow's undeveloped periphery. The dark fields that frame Lenin's figure create a directional movement within the image, suggesting that the march of socialist urbanization was set to continue. They also indicate the wings of an airplane, placing the reader in the cockpit.

This frontispiece was the work of the German Communist *photomonteur* John Heartfield, who had visited the Soviet Union to witness and contribute to the development of the USSR.[1] Describing his experience to the German press after his return, he underlined the tactical importance of images such as his montage for *USSR in Construction*. 'Every scrap of printed paper, every line of text, every book cover,' he wrote, 'must be of use in the great struggle for the only path that can save us — the path shown by the Communist Party.'[2] Unashamed of the propaganda value of his work, Heartfield enlisted his image of Moscow in an ongoing project for the construction of a city and a society that might manifest new, socialist relationships. By 1931, he was able to appropriate photographs of realized buildings to demonstrate the achievements and future prospects of Soviet architecture. These buildings owe a debt to the projects that had been proposed long before Heartfield's visit. For new Moscow was born earlier — first in pictures, then in space. But the spectacle of socialist Moscow was not simply a collection of images; rather, it was

John Heartfield, *Montage of Lenin over Moscow*, 1931

an attempt to create socialist relationships between people that was mediated by images.[3] The visions for Moscow that emerged after the October Revolution demonstrate a range of attempts to configure socialist relationships as architects sought to follow the Communist Party's unpredictable path.

'THE SKYSCRAPER IS A REALITY FOR THE USSR'. In the early years of Soviet power, the skyscraper emerged as a powerful symbol of technological and social modernization. The building type condensed a long-standing interest in American culture and technology in Russia. Even before the October Revolution, the poet Aleksandr Blok had written 'as coal becomes a diamond, Russia becomes a new America,' conflating development with *Amerikanizm*.[4] In the early 1920s, the skyscraper symbolized the aspirations for an approach to urban and architectural development that would fuse American technology and Soviet planning.

The first project for a socialist tower originated in Petrograd, the Russified designation St Petersburg acquired during World War I. In 1919, the artist Vladimir Tatlin began work on his so-called *Monument to the Third International*, constructing a model in a workshop of the former Imperial Academy of Fine Arts. Composed of two ascending spirals, Tatlin's monument housed a series of government ministries in volumes suspended from the steel structure. Rotating at various speeds, these spaces ensured that the new monument would be a functional object. Antennas and film projectors crowned the structure, indicating the importance of agitation to the project. While Tatlin published images of his *Monument* towering over an urban landscape, he never specified a site for the building with any certainty. This was a strategic decision, for the centre of Soviet power was shifting away from Petrograd to Moscow as he worked on the project

While Tatlin's tower would be realized only in model form, its presentation of a government building as a dynamic structure of steel, glass and radio antennas would have a significant impact on Moscow's architectural imaginary. The 'Spectacle for the Third International', a proposal for a mass demonstration conceived by Aleksandr Vesnin and the painter Liubov Popova, echoed the forms and aims of Tatlin's *Monument*. Vesnin and Popova orchestrated a contest between a 'city of capitalism' and a 'city of the future' that was to take place on Khodynskoe Field in Moscow. The 'city of capitalism' is made up of solid, block-like forms; the 'city of the future', the socialist city, is composed of openwork flywheels, crane-like arms, and radio masts. Vesnin and Popova's new city drew on the forms of Tatlin's *Monument*, suggesting that the future, socialist city would be composed of rational technical forms. Vesnin explored the potential of these forms in a series of stage designs in the following years, but the project he submitted with his brothers, Viktor and Leonid, to the Palace of Labour competition of 1923 offered a radically new image of Moscow's architecture. The Vesnins' Palace, intended to be the new seat of the Soviet government, avoided the

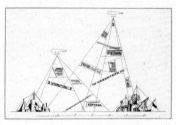

Aleksandr Vesnin and Lyubov Popova, *Spectacle for the Third International*, Moscow, 1921

symmetry and monumentality of traditional state architecture. Its form emerged from the stark rhythm of its reinforced concrete frame and the functional distribution of volumes. Like Tatlin's tower, antennas and screens were incorporated into the design. In 1927, the architect and theorist Moisei Ginzburg identified the building as the first mature statement of Constructivism in architecture. This was not only for the rationality of its structural system. More important, Ginzburg claimed, was the fact that the Vesnin brothers had created a 'new social organism' — one that was manifest in the logic and clarity of the architectural design.

The skyscraper figured prominently in the remarkable but short-lived publication *Izvestia ASNOVA* (ASNOVA News), which was published by the Association of New Architects. In the first and only issue of 1926, El Lissitzky, writing under a pseudonym, asserted that 'for the USSR, the skyscraper is now not a problem, but a reality'.[5] Vladimir Krinsky's project for a skyscraper for the Council of National Economy in Moscow, which was illustrated in the magazine, seemed to confirm this statement. The key feature of *Izvestia ASNOVA*, however, was El Lissitzky's so-called *Wolkenbügel* ('Cloud Iron') project. Imagined as a counter-model to the American skyscraper, Lissitzky's 'Cloud Iron' sought to achieve a 'spatial equilibrium' by balancing horizontal and vertical elements. Recalling the floating forms of his earlier Proun paintings, the 'Cloud Iron' appears to hover above old Moscow. This effect is heightened in a photomontage of the structure at Nikitskie Vorota, where Lissitzky's structure straddles the street, transforming traffic islands into functional spaces. Lissitzky intended his project to be reproducible and provided a map for a ring of such structures to surround the city's historic core.

The proposals of Lissitzky, Krinsky and the Vesnin brothers were, to a certain degree, at odds with the official approach to urban planning adopted by Moscow Soviet in the early 1920s. Alexey Shchusev played a significant role in the development of the plan for 'New Moscow', which was published in 1923. Despite its name, this document sought to preserve Moscow's historical character, rather than reimagine its form and structure. The articulation of new transportation networks and the provision of urban green space were among Shchusev's key priorities. In the city centre, Shchusev sought to maintain the mix of old and new structures, thereby safeguarding Moscow's unique appearance. While 'New Moscow' foresaw the provision of many new buildings and workers' quarters, it was often criticized for its retrospective character. One writer published a critique of the plan in the *Izvestia* newspaper, writing that 'Moscow is not a museum of antiquities, nor is it a city of tourists, nor Venice, nor Pompeii'.[6]

The retrospective nature of Shchusev's 'New Moscow' had a definite impact on the first high-rise for Moscow with prospects for realization: Grigorii Barkhin's headquarters for the *Izvestia* newspaper on Strastnaia Square. Barkhin's initial project of 1925 drew heavily on the Vesnin brothers' Palace of Labour competition entry. Composed of a broad base and a tower block, it was articulated by the strong rhythm of its structural frame. The upper floors of Barkhin's tower included cantilevered balconies that wrap around the corner, recalling precedents such as Walter Gropius's project for the Chicago Tribune competition of 1922. But height restrictions included in the 'New Moscow' plan forced Barkhin to alter the basic features of his design. The tower was removed, and only the base remained. During this modification, Barkhin added circular windows for the editors' offices. When the building was complete, the editors of *Sovremennaia arkhitektura* (Contemporary Architecture, *CA*), the magazine published by the Constructivist Union of Contemporary Architects, offered a critical appraisal. They noted that the circular windows seemed to be decorative imitations of ocean liners. They also criticized the insertion of balconies adjacent to production floors, precisely where they were unnecessary. In place of a 'fashionable use of the "Constructivist style"', the editors demanded an organic architecture 'that creates new social types'.[7] Barkhin's *Izvestia* building, it seemed to the Constructivists, offered only the image of a new Moscow without the corresponding social content.

THE DISAPPEARING CITY. In the second half of the 1920s, just as real construction was resuming pre-revolutionary levels, many Soviet archi-

Model of Ivan Leonidov's 'Lenin Institute of Library Sciences', First Exhibition of Modern Architecture, Moscow, 1927

tects sought a critical distance from the spatial matrix of Moscow in an effort to imagine new social relationships. While many sought to insert skyscrapers within the existing fabric of Moscow, others adopted an approach to design that undermined traditional relationships between architecture and the city. Others experimented in the relative freedom afforded by the undeveloped periphery. For some, the future of the socialist city seemed to depend on the disappearance of Moscow itself.

The architectural studios of VKhUTEMAS, the Higher Art and Technical Studios, were laboratories for the imagination of new Moscow. Ivan Leonidov, one of the school's most inventive students, offered an innovative approach to architecture in his diploma project for a 'Lenin Institute of Library Sciences'. Nominally intended for Sparrow Hills in southwestern Moscow, Leonidov's project exceeded the confines of its site.

Composed of a circular platform, a vertical book stack and a spherical auditorium, the library institute appears to extend in all directions. Moisei Ginzburg described how Leonidov's project demonstrated a 'reorganization of the very understanding of space in the city'.[8] The library institute would feature prominently both in the 'First Exhibition of Contemporary Architecture' in Moscow in 1927 and in the international press in the following years.

Nikolay Sokolov sought escape from Moscow in his project for a resort hotel of 1928. Presented in the pages of CA in a series of photomontages, Sokolov's resort was intended to spatialize a proletarian relationship to nature and leisure. But Sokolov resisted the type of the bourgeois hotel, which he described as the 'old functions of the capitalist apartment plus the old functions of the high-society club plus the luxurious decorativeness of its means'.[9] Sokolov proposed instead a series of cylindrical residential units that could be dispersed throughout the natural landscape. This new resort sought to fully integrate buildings with nature, thereby demonstrating a social ownership of land and the availability of restorative leisure to all. In this way, Sokolov wrote, 'the small resort hotel becomes a weapon in the struggle of the class that created it.'[10]

For some architects, the communal house represented a radical response to the traditional city. Communal houses had emerged with the success of the October Revolution, largely by settling multiple families into large bourgeois apartment buildings. By the late 1920s, Constructivist architects sought to develop new social types of housing that might foster new social relationships. Experiments such as Moisei

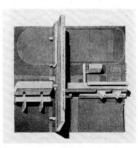

Mikhail Barshch and Viacheslav Vladimirov, *Experimental Design for a Communal House*, 1929

Ginzburg and Ignatii Milinis's Narkomfin Building (1928-30) explored the potential for the provision of social services within a unified block on a small scale. The theoretical projects published in the pages of CA demonstrated a new conception of the relationship between building and city. The proposal for a communal house for 1,680 people by Mikhail Barshch and Viacheslav Vladimirov of 1929 was among the most radical projects for collectivization. Including single-cell dwellings for adults and a separate children's sector, Barshch and Vladimirov's building articulated social functions in a new way. The building incorporated sports facilities, a library, a cafeteria, a kindergarten, a school, a gymnasium and a wide range of other facilities. In effect, the project proposed a new model of settlement distinct from the traditional neighbourhood — the communal house replaced the city as the framework for social life.

In other projects, Constructivist architects imagined not only an escape from Moscow, but predicted the withering of its historical core. The competition for a 'Green City' outside Moscow of 1929-1930 offered Moisei Ginzburg and Mikhail Barshch an opportunity to demonstrate the potential of new forms of socialist settlement to counteract the historical city. Their project for a satellite city of 100,000 was composed of linear, ribbon-like bands of settlement. Modest row houses and cultural facilities are strewn throughout the landscape — the traditional concepts of the street and the building had disappeared entirely. Ginzburg and Barshch considered their project as a starting point for the general reconstruction of Moscow, a task they understood as the 'unloading of the great accumulation of buildings, objects, and masses'.[11] For them, the spectacle of socialist Moscow was a vanishing act.

A MODEL OF STALIN'S REVOLUTION. The buildings featured in John Heartfield's photomontage for *USSR in Construction* were only distantly related to the radical urban and architectural concepts advanced by Ginzburg, Barshch, and others. The Usacheva district, while providing much-needed housing, remained fundamentally tied to traditional concepts of architecture and the city. The image of the district seemed to amplify the text of a speech made by Lazar Kaganovich on the reconstruction of Moscow that was summarized in the same issue of *USSR in Construction*. In June 1931, Kaganovich, the chair of Moscow Soviet and Stalin's closest architectural adviser, had asserted that all cities in the USSR had become socialist with the success of the revolution, thereby obviating the need for new forms of settlement.[12] This speech ended an intensive period of urbanistic debate. Following the 'Green City' competition, Le Corbusier was invited to submit proposals for the development of Moscow. His 'Response to Moscow' amounted to nothing less than a complete reorganization of the urban structure into functional zones — a prefiguration of his 'Ville Radieuse'.[13] Kaganovich's speech neutralized the radical interventions proposed by

Le Corbusier and others. A year earlier, the Party had precluded experiments in radical collectivity, effectively putting a halt to the social vision of communal houses such as Barshch and Vladimirov's. In decree after decree, the Party introduced new requirements for architects. When Heartfield described the need to follow 'the path shown by the Communist Party', he neglected to mention just how circuitous the path might be.

The competition for the Palace of the Soviets manifested the increasing dominance of the Party in cultural life. The project for a new seat of the Soviet government was initially greeted with enthusiasm both within the USSR and abroad. But to the surprise of the international architectural community, the jury of the first open competition awarded prizes not to any of the radically innovative proposals, but rather to a neo-Renaissance project by Ivan Zholtovskii, a stone-clad building by the unknown Anglo-American architect Hector Hamilton, and a design featuring a tower and monumental sculpture by Boris Iofan. The jury imposed new requirements on submissions to the following round of competition, asking that entries incorporate both modern technologies and historical precedents in their forms.[14] This demand challenged the Soviet Union's leading architects to either abandon the course of radical innovation or be left behind in the Party's vision for architecture.

The Palace and the need to assimilate historical precedents that it entailed were a constant presence in the minds of Soviet architects. Its monumentality and fusion of advanced technology with historical forms served as a model for the profession. A new, experimental approach

Lev Rudnev's project for the Red Army Theatre, Architectural Exhibition on Gorky Street, Moscow, 1933

to historical precedents became evident in a range of projects for Moscow in the mid-1930s. This diversity was the subject of an exhibition of architecture that took place in the shop windows on Gorky Street in the centre of Moscow in October 1933.[15] Banners calling for 'the decisive reconstruction of the architectural form of Moscow' hung across the street, while projects for public buildings filled the vitrines. One window showed work by

Ivan Fomin juxtaposed with portraits of Lenin and Kaganovich. Another featured Lev Rudnev's monumental projects for the Ministry of Defence. Relief sculptures of tank treads identified Rudnev's buildings and illustrated his attempt at creating an *architecture parlante*. One photograph of the Gorky Street exhibition depicts an unidentified spectator gazing at a project for the Red Army Theatre. While the viewer examines the building's colonnade, a portrait of Stalin looks out of the shop window, seeming to hold the spectator in his gaze.

Other projects of the 1930s sought to refashion both Moscow's historic core and its overall form. The first round of competition for the Headquarters of the Commissariat of Heavy Industry (Narkomtiazhprom) of 1934 witnessed a striking diversity of form. Leonidov's project, one of the most

Panorama of Moscow developed on the basis of the 1935 plan, 1936

celebrated, combined three towers of varying profiles with a broad tribune that was to extend the entire length of Red Square. Fomin based his project on the coffered vaults of Ancient-Roman basilicas. Konstantin Melnikov's project drew explicitly on industrial imagery, using circular, bearing-like forms as portals for a building composed of intersecting triangular volumes. The document that structured the many sites of experiment within the city was the 1935 Plan for the Reconstruction of Moscow. The main orientation of the plan had been articulated four years earlier by Kaganovich: its aim was not to abandon the city's historical form, but rather to heighten and emphasize its features.[16] The 1935 plan specified the widening of streets and the reconstruction of residential blocks with new, higher buildings. The planners who drafted the document were equally concerned with the technological modernization of the city as with its beautification. They imagined a city of boulevards and monuments. This vision was conveyed in powerful form in the end-paper illustrations that accompanied the official publication of the plan.[17] Like Heartfield's image of 1931, this panorama of socialist Moscow depicts the city from the air. But here, the draftsman has imagined the city as completed according to the provisions of the Plan of 1935. The Palace of the Soviets is complete, monumental housing blocks surround verdant courtyards, vertical monuments frame and articulate broad boulevards, and the entire urban fabric is ordered according to the logic of Party-led development. Lenin is visible not as a shadow pointing to the future, but as a sculpture atop the Palace, gazing out over the city. This dream image of Moscow is anchored to reality by the airplane wing at the lower left corner. Like Heartfield's image of 1931, it too places the reader in the cockpit, offering a different, but equally spectacular, view.

1   For details of Heartfield's trip to the USSR, see Maria Gough, 'Back in the USSR: John Heartfield, Gustav Klucis, and the Medium of Soviet Propaganda', *New German Critique* 36, no. 2 (2009), 133-83.

2   John Heartfield, 'Heimkehr [1932]', in *John Heartfield: Der Schnitt entlang der Zeit*, ed. Roland März (Dresden: Verlag der Kunst, 1981), 285.

3   This is a paraphrase of one of Guy Debord's theses on the society of the spectacle. See Guy Debord, *The Society of the Spectacle*, trans. Donald Nicholson-Smith (New York: Zone Books, 1995), 12.

4   Alexander Blok, 'Vozmezdie', in *Sobrannye sochinenii*, ed. V. N. Orlova, A. A. Surkov and K. I. Chukovskii (Moscow: Gosudarstvennoe izdatel'stvo khudozhestvennoi literatury, 1960), 298. On the Soviet interest in America, see Jean-Louis Cohen, 'America: A Soviet Ideal', *AA Files 5* (1984), 32-40.

5   Lissitzky adopted the pseudonym 'Enael' for this essay. See El Lissitzky, 'Neboskreby SSSR i Ameriki', *Izvestia ASNOVA*, no. 1 (1926), 3.

6   KN Afanas'ev and VE Khazanova (eds.), *Iz istorii sovetskoi arkhitektury, 1917-25 gg.: dokumenty i materialy* (Moscow: Izd-vo Akademii nauk SSSR, 1963), 50.

7   '[Comment on *Izvestia* Headquarters]', *Sovremennaia arkhitektura* 3, no. 4 (1928), 132.

8   M Ia Ginzburg, 'Itogi i perspektivy SA', *Sovremennaia arkhitektura* 2, no. 4-5 (1927), 116.

9   N Sokolov, 'Opyt arkhitekturnogo myshleniia: tema: kurortnaia gostinitsa', *Sovremennaia arkhitektura* 4, no. 3 (1929), 97.

10 Ibid., 98.

11 M Barshch and M Ia Ginzburg, 'Zelenyi gorod: Sotsialisticheskaia rekonstruktsiia Moskvy', *Sovremennaia arkhitektura* 5, no. 1-2 (1930), 17.

12 See L M Kaganovich, *Socialist Reconstruction of Moscow and Other Cities in the U.S.S.R.* (New York: International Publishers, 1931).

13 See Jean-Louis Cohen, *Le Corbusier and the Mystique of the USSR: Theories and Projects for Moscow, 1928-36* (Princeton: Princeton University Press, 1992), 127-63.

14 See Richard Anderson, *Russia: Modern Architectures in History* (London: Reaktion Books, 2015), 147-81.

15 See the illustrations to E Kriger, 'Obrashchenie k arkhitektoru', *Arkhitektura SSSR* 2, no. 1 (1934), 8-11.

16 See Harald Bodenschatz and Christiane Post, *Städtebau im Schatten Stalins: Die internationale Suche nach der sozialistischen Stadt in der Sowjetunion 1929-1935* (Berlin: Braun, 2003).

17 Ia S Tsvankin (ed). *General'nyi plan rekonstruktsii goroda Moskvy: 1. Postanovleniia i materialy* (Moscow: Moskovskii rabochii, 1936).

LISSITZKY'S 'AMERIKANIZM'

JEAN-LOUIS COHEN

Trained as he was in Germany before 1914, it is through Germany that El Lissitzky discovered American architecture after the revolution. In 1922 he published the ephemeral journal *Veshch/Gegenstand/Objet* with the writer Ilya Ehrenburg. The first page of the third and last issue featured, paired with Kazimir Malevich's black square, an image of an American

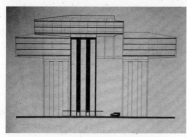

El Lissitzky, *Design for the Cloud Iron in Moscow*, view from Strastnoy Boulevard, 1925

railway engine, complete with its snow plough, and a further issue devoted to America was announced.[1] Weimar Germany, which in the years since the signing of the 1922 Rapallo agreement by Soviet foreign minister Georgy Chicherin and his German counterpart Walther Rathenau had fostered close industrial, military and cultural relationships with the USSR, became an indispensable filter for the Russian perception of American architecture, as the new regime would not be recognized by the United States before 1933.

In the transfer of American types and models to the USSR through Germany, the role of Lissitzky is essential; he can be considered as a travelling salesman, importing them towards the East, while bringing fragments of Soviet experience to the West. His 1924 *Wolkenbügel*, or 'Cloud Iron', proposed for several locations on Moscow's boulevard ring, is an explicit attempt at opposing the rational, horizontal structures of the eclectic American skyscrapers. His 1925 essay on '"Amerikanizm" in European Architecture', reprinted here, is most explicit in its critique of buildings whose 'living skeleton' has been unduly camouflaged. Symptomatically, when he considers that 'Europe today is more American than America itself,' he subscribes to the previous year's aphorism of Leon Trotsky, according to whom 'Americanized Bolshevism will triumph and smash imperialist Americanism.'[2]

In 1926, Lissitzky published in the monthly journal *Stroitelnaya promyshlennost*, a regular chronicle titled 'America in Construction' in which

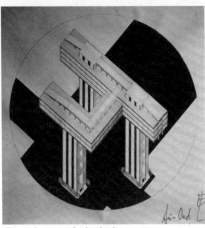

El Lissitzky, *Design for the Cloud Iron in Moscow*, aerial view, 1925

he analysed the skeleton of industrial structures and skyscrapers. Though he regarded notions introduced by Louis Sullivan and Frank Lloyd Wright as positive, Lissitzky asserted that the centre of gravity of the new architecture was no longer located in America, but in the work of the Taut brothers, of Ludwig Mies van der Rohe, and of Auguste Perret, while the problem of the skyscraper was seriously examined in 'our Union'.[3] This had been the message of the single issue of *Izvestia ASNOVA* he published the same year, together with Nikolay Ladovsky, with a layout he designed, in which a parallel was drawn between skyscrapers in the USSR and America.[4]

Lissitzky would pursue his chronicle with the article 'The Architect's Eye', in which he analysed the vision shaped by Berlin architect Erich Mendelsohn in his 1926 book *Amerika, das Bilderbuch eines Architekten*.[5] Based in large part on photographs taken by Mendelsohn himself, this album became for him a 'dramatic movie', a book 'which needs to be read held high above one's head'. It was finally an 'America seen not from a distance, but from the inside'. He suggested that it would 'greet the eye of the architect, showing us things we know in a more profound manner', but also mourned the fact that 'real progress, real change in the principles and forms of the division of space is still very rare,' and that 'every object grows by outbursts, as in a tropical forest, depriving its neighbour of air and light, devouring it.'[6]

Lissitzky would remain a significant contributor to the period's fashionable *Amerikanizm*, not only recycling a photograph of night-time Broadway by Fritz Lang published by Mendelsohn, for one of his collages on the theme of sport, but also borrowing the Berlin architect's point of view in what would remain for decades the only account of Moscow's new architecture: his volume *Rußland, die Rekonstruktion der Architektur in der Sowjetunion*, published in Vienna in 1930.[7]

1 *Veshch/Gegenstand/Objet 3* (May 1922), 1.

2 Lev D. Trotsky, 'K voprosu of perspektivakh mirovogo razvitia', *Izvestia* (5 August 1924).

3 El Lissitzky, 'Arkhitektura zheleznoy i zhelezobetonnoy ramy', *Stroitelnaya promyshlennost* 1 (January 1926), 59-63.

4 Nikolay Ladovsky, 'Neboskreby SSSR i Ameriki', *Izvestia ASNOVA* 1 (1926)

5 Erich Mendelsohn, *Amerika, das Bilderbuch eines Architekten* (Berlin: Mosse, 1926).

6 El Lissitzky, 'Glaz arkhitektora', *Stroitelnaya promyshlennost* 2 (February 1926), 144-6.

7 El Lissitzky, *Rußland, die Rekonstruktion der Architektur in der Sowjetunion* (Vienna: Anton Schroll u. Co., 1930), 72, 77, 84, 85.

'AMERIKANIZM' IN EUROPEAN ARCHITECTURE (1925)

EL LISSITZKY

From El Lissitzky, *Life, Letters, Texts*
Translated by Sophie Lissitzky-Küppers

In the Old World — in Europe — the words 'America' and 'American' conjure up ideas of something ultraperfect, rational, utilitarian, universal. All these notions are alien to the old artists of Europe. What has any European ever sought in America in respect of art or culture or anything else — apart from dollars? Only when both victors and vanquished found themselves, as a result of the war, at the American pawnbroker's did Europe discover America a second time: and once the Americans themselves had swarmed over to Europe, they saw their own country with new eyes. Harold Loeb, the editor of *Broom*, wrote 'For a nation to create art, it must have its ideal, its god. America's god is the dollar: so its architecture has produced skyscrapers, its sculpture produces machines, its pictorial art is the cinema.' Matthew Josephson discovered the great anonymous poetry of America — the verses and advertisements written in lights in the night sky of Chicago and New York.

Meanwhile, Europe was lacking the specialists she required to repair the ravages of war. Since the time of the Renaissance she had fostered a guild of master craftsmen known as 'artists', who have survived up to the present time. These men did not know how to meet the requirements of the day, and it was precisely in America that Europe discovered a new guild of men who were working to fulfil the day-to-day, the hour-to-hour, demands of the present time — the engineers. Thus to the European mind New York became the new Athens, Manhattan the Acropolis, and the skyscrapers the Parthenon. It is true that New York itself knew nothing of this discovery. There they continue to build their temples to the Greek gods over subway stations, with the firm conviction that they are more beautiful than the original ones because they are ten times bigger. In New York and Chicago, engineers invented and constructed the fantastic steel skeletons of skyscrapers fifty storeys high, but the artist-architects, trained at the ancient Paris academy, clothed this living skeleton so skilfully with ostentatious embellishments that it was twenty years later before Europe recognized the crux of the matter.

It was where work went on without the architectonic embellishments, where the engineer clearly defined his task, conscientiously observed the conditions imposed by his material and fulfilled the requirements of his construction, in the grain belt of the Western States and Canada, that there appeared these elevators and silos which so astounded European architects. And there in the West originated the works of Frank Lloyd Wright, America's only architect, who dared to discard all textbook precepts and to create a new type of dwelling, which has revealed him as the father of contemporary architecture.

Before the war the most intense architectural activity went on in Germany, but this architecture was either à la Iron Fist or à la Gretchen. Both were swept away by the war. The prolonged standstill in new building, and the unprecedented growth of the towns, produced a housing crisis in Germany. Germany had destroyed Belgium and Northern France; all this had to be rebuilt. The neutral countries — Holland, Denmark and Switzerland — had for a time profited from the war and made tremendous progress in their building development. These vast requirements compelled people to reconsider all the problems of architecture from a new viewpoint.

The new generation of architects began with the basic principles of construction. Up to this time a house had been built by the same methods that were employed in Babylon and Egypt. Here the mortar is mixed on the building-site itself and the bricklayer erects his wall by sticking the individual bricks together, like a needlewoman embroidering a towel with cross-stitch. This method served its purpose well enough in the days of princes and potentates, whose portraits were painted by an equally primitive method. Nowadays when a man requires a portrait of himself he goes to the photographer and has a dozen photographs produced without delay. This man must also have his house built in a different way. After all, a house is a device for living in, just as a car or an aeroplane is a device for travelling in. For this reason building norms and construction times must be worked out, so that building can be transferred to mass-production factories and houses ordered from a catalogue.

Prefabricated parts, which only need to be fitted together, should be delivered to the site. America was the first to solve this problem in a practical way. The present record for erecting a small one-family house is eight hours for assembly of the parts, and the house is ready to be occupied within two days. The new generation in Europe is now struggling to adopt these ideas. The ideological campaign which has been waged for several years is already bearing fruit: at the building-exhibition in Dresden this summer, the architect Lüdecke built a prototype of the prefabricated house for industrial mass-production. Mass construction methods require these large, smooth slabs of wall, the rectangular shapes, the flat roofs — in fact, everything that is characteristic of the new geometric style.

Inseparably linked with the method of construction is the question of the material used in building. To construct a brick wall by machine at the factory and then transport it to the site to erect it there would, of course, be absurd. Our age has created a new structural material — concrete. Houses can be cast from it as statues are cast from bronze, but as far as dwellings are concerned it has a number of disadvantages. Experiments are now in progress everywhere, to try and invent new materials, which will be light, easy to mould, provide good heat insulation, and so on; and in this field Europe is beginning to outstrip America. In solving this problem the main effort lies in the creation of a new form.

As a result of new methods and new materials, a new kind of construction is emerging. 'American' techniques have opened the eyes of European architects to the fact that the new material has to be assembled in accordance with new principles in order to withstand strains and loads imposed on it. The new architects, in striving to create a new form, have realized the necessity for showing its basic construction openly and honestly. In formulating and solving these problems Europe today is more American than America itself.

In the new constructions the main achievement has been to free the walls from having the sole responsibility of supporting the weight of the superstructure. The walls have the function of a casserole; they serve merely as a protection against the weather; apertures are simply cut out of them for the windows, but the entire weight is borne by the special skeleton. European architects, striving like all artists to achieve simplicity and clarity, have devoted their whole attention to these basic principles. Highly intricate compositional patterns are fairly common, but modern man, travelling by tram, road or railway, goes past them without even noticing them. Large masses, clear and unequivocal, serve as key points for finding one's bearings inside a town. In this respect the design for an office-block by the Berlin architect Mies van der Rohe is a characteristic example. Starting off with his material (reinforced concrete) and his design, he proceeds to create a house in which walls — in the original meaning of the word — do not exist. We see only large horizontal strips — unbroken stretches of filing-cabinets on the inside, alternating with unbroken stretches of window above. Even more powerful and more direct is the impression made by the reinforced concrete airship-hangars at Orly, near Paris. These are not the work of an artist-architect, but of an engineer-constructor, Freyssinet, a man possessed of that same French spirit which inspired Eiffel. In a hangar of this size there would be room for a whole row of St Basil's cathedrals.

We can see how special types of buildings have been conceived. They are the result of the swift growth of modern towns where three segments have clearly crystallized: (1) the commercial quarter, the 'City', which is teeming with several million people by day, while only a few score watchmen remain there at night; (2) the industrial quarter, the factory districts, where work goes on uninterrupted round the clock; and (3) the residential quarter. Each of these areas has produced its own type of house: skyscraper, factory and apartment-block.

Europe is adopting American principles, developing them in a new way. From this point of view it is interesting that of the huge number of entries submitted to the competition for a skyscraper design, organized by the *Chicago Tribune*, only a few European architects, for example, the Dane Lundberg-Folm, and the Germans Gropius, May, and Bruno Taut, attempted a form suited to American construction. America herself had covered her steel skeleton with endless metres of Gothic and rosette-like ornaments.

Europe is ahead of America in one respect, namely in dealing with the housing problem, and more particularly with workers' housing. In this field Holland has surpassed other countries. Model complexes can be seen in Rotterdam; very modest, almost austere as seen from the street, open along their whole frontage to the courtyard at the back, which is thus transformed into an enclosed space with little playgrounds for the children and gardens for relaxation. Europe adopts the organized, practical ideas of America, but clarifies and defines them. This process must be applied not only to exterior architecture, but also to an even greater extent to interior design.

The truth is that here Europe makes it her aim to meet the demands of economy, strict utility and hygiene. Architects are convinced that through the new design and planning of the house they are actively participating in the organizing of a new consciousness.

We had occasion to meet a number of great masters of the new architecture in Europe and were convinced of the difficulty of their position. They are surrounded by a chauvinistic, reactionary, individualistic society, to whom these men, with their international mental horizon, their revolutionary activity and their collective thinking, are alien and hostile. That is why they all follow the trend of events in our country so attentively and all believe that the future belongs not to the USA but to the USSR.

THE SOCIALIST VATICAN
DEYAN SUDJIC

When you look at Europe's capital cities, you see, spelled out in physical form, the nature of the ideas that brought them into being. Today's London is the fruit of unintended consequences. Its skyline is dictated by a market economy, distorted by the demands placed on it by politicians who have tried to shift the provision of civic amenities on to private finance. Canary Wharf, the second biggest financial centre in Europe, exists as the result of an accident, built using incentives designed not to encourage the construction of skyscrapers, but to support job-creating industrial sheds. Paris has a historic centre built for Napoleon III by Baron Haussmann in an attempt to create the image of an imperial capital, though not successful enough to discourage the Paris Commune or the Prussian invasion of 1870. Moscow has different roots. With the Kremlin at its heart, it still has a structure bequeathed by a medieval autocracy. Since 1917 it has been the subject of a concerted effort to make it the capital not just of Russia or of the Soviet Union, but of a new world order. A capital shaped not by the market, but by an idea of what a city could be.

When the Alekseevsky convent was built on a water meadow just outside the Kremlin wall in 1347, Moscow was a city still being fought over by Poles, Lithuanians and Russians. The city was just a couple of centuries old, and still had memories of being burned to the ground by the Tartars. Over seven centuries this particular site reveals the violent shifts in the nature of not just Moscow, but Russia too.

The remains of the convent were demolished to make way for the Cathedral of Christ the Saviour, the largest Orthodox church in the world, paid for with the kopeks of Russian peasants dropped into collecting boxes all over Russia, as a celebration of national deliverance from Napoleon's troops. Tsar Alexander I had commissioned Alexander Vitberg to design a cathedral of a scale and grandeur that would reflect Russia's ambition to be seen as a mighty and expansive state. With a dome more than 750 feet high, it would have been twice the size of the Vatican. But there were doubts about its feasibility. After Vitberg was accused of embezzlement and exiled to Siberia, Alexander's successor, Nicholas I, handed the project over to another architect, Konstantin Ton, who redesigned it in a more traditional Russian style, and on a more modest scale. Nevertheless, at 360 feet to the top of the cross on its biggest dome, it was still as tall as London's St Paul's. When it was finally completed, Tchaikovsky wrote the 1812 overture in celebration. A taper lit at one of its altars was believed to bring good fortune, provided that you could get it home without it blowing out. Easter services attracted thousands of worshippers to the vast white marble structure.

Stalin dynamited the church in 1931. He was determined to recast the centre of Moscow, and he wanted the site for the Palace of the Soviets, the symbol of his regime. Under the supervision of Stalin's close politicalally,

Photo of the destruction of the original Church of Christ the Saviour in Moscow, Russia, 1931

Vyacheslav Molotov, a competition was organized to find a designer. The brief was to produce a 'monumental structure outstanding in its architectural formulation'. Molotov's men searched the world for suitable candidates. Walter Gropius and Hans Poelzig, competitors for the chance to build Hitler's Reichsbank just two years earlier, took part alongside Erich Mendelsohn, Auguste Perret, Le Corbusier, Naum Gabo and three Soviet architectural teams. The eventual winner after several rounds was Boris Iofan, a well-connected architect from Ukraine, who was not yet forty.

After studying in Odessa, Iofan had spent ten years in Rome working in the studio of Armando Brasini, the man who became close to Mussolini and worked in Libya and on the replanning of Rome. He joined the Italian Communist Party while he was abroad, and was almost certainly a Soviet secret agent. His design, guided by what he went on to describe as Stalin's genius, would have been as tall as the Empire State Building, topped by a representation of Lenin, pointing at the Kremlin, that itself would have overshadowed the Statue of Liberty. Together reaching 500 metres high, the scale would have been without historical precedent. In this model, there were echoes of his former mentor, Brasini, who had also participated in the first round of the Palace of the Soviets competition. It was in his

Boris Iofan, *The Palace of the Soviets*, 1933-7

Iofan's workshop engaged in drawing the project of the Palace of the Soviets, 1930s

design that the giant representation of Lenin was first drafted. Brasini had already explored this essentially classical idea more than once. In 1916 he had designed a monument to Dante in Rome in the form of a lighthouse crowned by a statue of the poet. He returned to the same theme after Mussolini came to power, this time as a skyscraper topped with an outsize representation of a Roman soldier.

Stalin asked the finalists to incorporate 'the best of the past, with modern technology'. To this end, Iofan teamed up with officially approved architects Vladimir Shchuko and Vladimir Gelfreikh to build the project. But it was Iofan that Stalin chose to rebuild Moscow in his image. Living in the House on the Embankment, the sprawling city within the city he had built himself to house the party elite, Iofan could have watched the dynamiting of the cathedral from the window of his apartment. He might have looked on as ill-fated residents were marched away by the NKVD on many nights during the purges. The survivors would ask the doormen for the names of the disappeared.

Justifying the destruction of the cathedral, Iofan coolly claimed that the old church was 'huge, and cumbersome, looking like a cake, or a samovar [...] which symbolise [d] the power and the taste of the lords of old Moscow'. The demolition was supervised by the secret police who made sure that the gangs of workmen stripping the gold from the domes handed over the spoils to the state (the yield was almost half a ton of bullion). Some of the marble and the granite from the exterior was salvaged for reuse in the building of the Lenin Library. The icons from the main altar were sold to Eleanor Roosevelt. But much of the statuary and the commemorative stained glass were deliberately destroyed. Those still brave enough to challenge Stalin's determination to destroy every trace protested angrily. Several priests who tried to salvage religious relics were summarily shot, while two technicians who refused to take part in dynamiting the remains of the hulk were sent to the gulags. Remembering the sacrifices of the Russian people in defeating an invader from Western Europe was off the agenda.

Having destroyed the Holy Saviour, the leaders of the new Moscow started on building its replacement in 1935. 'Why is the podium raised so little above the hall?' Stalin demanded. 'It must be higher. There must be no chandeliers, the illumination must come from indirect light.' The main hall was increased to a capacity of 21,000 seats, under a 100-metres-high-dome. It was ringed by six smaller halls, each thematically expressing a section of the six-part oath Stalin took when he succeeded Lenin, including the Stalin Constitution Hall, and the Hall of the Building of Socialism, as well as a Museum of World Revolution. In the main auditorium, speakers would have addressed the masses from a huge tribune, topped by a cluster of triumphant proletarians,

Iofan's perspective of the 416-metre Palace of the Soviets, 1937

carved in marble. The tower was designed in classical fashion, in three related parts. The base was to represent the precursors of socialism, the shaft of the tower Marx and Engels; the whole was crowned, of course, by the vision of Lenin. The tips of his fingers, 4 metres long, would have been lost in cloud on many days.

The ideological nature of Iofan's architecture was underscored by the Soviet pavilion at the Paris exposition of 1937, where Iofan's design confronted Albert Speer's German pavilion. Only the gigantic rendering of two workers wielding a hammer and sickle on the Soviet side, and the eagle and the swastika that topped Speer's stone pylon, made it immediately clear which was which. But from one point of view at least, the Palace of the Soviets was designed very differently from the monuments of

Albert Speer's Berlin. Rather than having an eye to its quality as a ruin, as Speer always did, in the Soviet Union Stalin's sycophants claimed that 'the centuries will not leave their mark on it, we shall build it so that it stands without ageing eternally.'

The Soviet Union, however, did not have the skill to build the structure. Accounts of the troubled construction of the original basilica, which had been plagued by flooding caused by a high water table and pressure from the river, were ignored by Stalin's cowed experts. Things seemed to go well at first. The foundations for the palace had been dug by the end of 1938 and work started on the steelwork. Clearing the entire site would have involved jacking up the Pushkin Museum, mounting it on huge rollers and moving it bodily out of the way, which the Politburo were fully prepared to do. By 1939, the road closures necessary to prepare for moving the museum out of the way had been announced. But the site was getting increasingly waterlogged and nothing that Iofan tried would solve the problem. The retaining walls were tanked with tar and lined with tombstones, but neither stopped the water rising for long. Many far more powerful men were executed as saboteurs for much less conspicuous failures, but Iofan evidently had a special rapport with Stalin that saved him from the gulag and the Lubyanka. He was left to build the Soviet pavilion at the New York World's Fair in 1939.

The process of building was as important for Stalin's purposes as the finished product. Moscow's shop windows in the 1930s and 1940s could offer little in the way of food, let alone consumer goods. But they were filled with images that depicted the Palace of the Soviets, in that distinctive dreamlike style favoured during the Stalin years. The dictator had himself portrayed as the fount of all this magnificence, its creative genius, infantilizing the Soviet Union in the process. The *Architecture of the USSR* May 1940 issue devoted twelve pages to Iofan, printing his picture next to the latest version of the Palace of the Soviets, with pages reproduced from his sketchbook showing watercolours of the Pantheon and the Roman amphitheatre at Syracuse. He was described as a master of Soviet architecture, and the piece documents the transformation of the conference hall from its original 1932 design to its final incarnation. In the first version, three concentric drums surround the dome. They sprout classical wings in the shape of twin crescents equipped with an endless procession of giant Corinthian columns flanking the entrance. After that came the tower, and the ever more colossal statue of Lenin. Almost every subsequent issue of the magazine is haunted by the shadowy presence of the Palace of the Soviets in one form or another. It is there in the background of the artists' impressions of every new scheme designed for central Moscow, a huge rocket, blocking out the light, all-seeing and inescapable.

It was only the German invasion of 1941 that stopped work. The palace's structural steel, by this time reaching as high as the eleventh floor, was dismantled for war use; Iofan and his models were transferred to a new studio on the eastern side of the Urals. After the war, Iofan returned to his apartment, and continued to work on the project, offering Stalin a number of options for its completion, none of which was adopted. Instead, Stalin decided on another project to transform Moscow by building a ring of high-rise towers that in their impact recalled some of the Constructivists' proposals from the 1920s, but used a very different architectural language, one that drew on Iofan's work for the Palace of the Soviets. The project to build eight towers was announced in 1947. Moscow State University, designed by Lev Rudnev, is the largest. Along with the Hotel Ukraina, the Ministry of Foreign Affairs, the Leningradskaya Hotel and three other towers, it was completed by 1952.

After Stalin's death, Khrushchev was ready to denounce the crimes of his predecessor in a closed session of the Communist Party of the Soviet Union. He turned the remains of the palace into the largest open-air swimming pool in the world, a perfect circle with a 100 metre diameter, presenting a less autocratic, more populist version of the Soviet system. From his increasingly shabby apartment, Iofan could again have looked down on a demolition site. This time, though, the destruction was of the project

N Granovsky, open-air swimming pool in the foundations of the Palace of the Soviets, c 1960

for which he had surrendered his integrity to the dictator of the twentieth century with more blood on his hands than Hitler. Iofan died in 1979. The Soviet Union had only another thirteen years left. In the last years of the Soviet Union, the pool closed and the water was drained. Even before the collapse of the old system, the state had given permission for a new church to be rebuilt on the site. The first post-Soviet mayor of Moscow, Yury Luzhkov, demolished the pool and began to build a replica of what Stalin had destroyed in one of the first and most conspicuous projects of his eighteen-year reign.

Phil Sayer, the Leningradskaya Hotel, Moscow, one of the seven Stalin towers, 2001

Emerging from Moscow's Kropotkinskaya metro station today, you pass the loafers drinking beer at the café table. You turn, and are confronted by a vision so dazzling that you can hardly see anything else. The five golden domes of the Cathedral of Christ the Saviour hurt the eyes, gleaming in the sun with a patina that seems to turn a vivid shade of turquoise.

A bronze relief frieze of figures runs around the exterior, charting Russian history. Warriors clutch their spears and bearded priests brandish the word of God, held aloft on metal tablets, like the digital cameras raised by supplicant tourists. The basilica is protected by a metal fence and ringed by elaborate cast-iron lamp posts, stone balustrades, and endless sequences of steps. It sits on a band of putty-coloured granite with a grey, rusticated stone base. Get closer and you discover that under the surface is a subterranean complex of ramps, roads and underground parking lots, all of which betray the whole gleaming confection as a faithful hallucination.

This is a replica of the church that Stalin destroyed. The bronze doors, sculptures, inscriptions, gaudy flower beds, lamp posts and carved stone are all the work of late-twentieth-century craftsmen. It is the kind of thing the people who make hyper-realistic effigies for Jeff Koons would do if left to themselves. The new church, like the memorial to Peter the Great across the river, is the product of the ex-mayor of Moscow, Luzhkov and the sculptor Zurab Tsereteli. Boris Yeltsin himself laid the foundation stone, and lay inside the completed basilica when he died. It is the church in which the five members of Pussy Riot filmed their 40-second protest against the connections between the Orthodox church and Putin's regime.

From the bedroom window of Iofan's apartment in the House on the Embankment, I once looked out to see the rebuilt domes of Christ the Saviour. The room had been neglected for decades. A plastic shower curtain had been slung over boxes of the architect's papers, but it did little to protect them from the dust caused by the workmen attempting to modernize the kitchen. There was a plaster maquette of the Lenin statue from the Palace of the Soviets under the desk. In one box I found sheaves of black-edged envelopes. I opened one to find that it contained a telegram from Stalin. Iofan's plea to have one of his assistants released from fighting the Germans so that he could join the evacuated architectural studio beyond the Urals had been granted. There were ancient photo albums. Here was Iofan shaking hands with Frank Lloyd Wright as they tour the Soviet pavilion that he designed for the New York's World Fair of 1939, an incongruous tribute to the proletarian revolution in Queens. The chaotic mess of books and papers, medals and ancient electrical appliances, felt like the residue of an entire system. Which is exactly what it was.

CHRONOLOGY

1915

NOVEMBER *We will soon have a famine. I advise you to buy ten pounds of bread and hide it. In the suburbs of Petrograd you can see well-dressed women begging on the streets. It is very cold. People have nothing to burn on their stoves. Here and there at night, they tear down the wooden fences. What has happened to the twentieth century? What has happened to civilization?* — Maxim Gorky

1917

15 MARCH Nicholas II, the last Russian Tsar, abdicates. He is removed from power by a provisional government led by Alexander Kerensky in the first of the year's two revolutions and held captive away from his capital, Petrograd. The Tsar and his family are executed in July the following year.

3 APRIL Lenin returns to Petrograd from exile in Switzerland with the cooperation of Germany, which is still at war with Russia, and Kerensky's provisional government that is standing by its treaty alliances with Britain and France. As the leader of the minority Bolsheviks, Lenin establishes the Politburo with Zinoviev, Trotsky, Sokolnikov, Stalin and Kamenev to plan a second seizure of power.

JUNE The Bolshevik manifesto for Moscow's first democratic local government election demands (1) *Universal municipal suffrage at age 18* (2) *Full autonomy from Petrograd* (3) *Nationalization of all urban land* (4) *Municipalization of local transport and utilities* (5) *A massive house building programme* (6) *Free elementary and vocational education, kindergartens, evening courses, and libraries* (7) *Universal health care, better hygiene and sanitation, free meals for children in need* (8) *Improved civic amenities — tarmac streets, lighting, sewers, water and parks — especially for Moscow's suburbs* (9) *Establishment of a city labour exchange, nurseries for working mothers, an eight-hour day, and paid holidays for all city employees* (10) *Replacement of the police with a popular militia controlled by the city* (11) *City annexation of Moscow's suburbs* (12) *Takeover by the city of private factories.*

Of the 647,000 votes cast, the Bolsheviks win only 75,000 and come fourth.

7 NOVEMBER After a brief armed coup in Petrograd lasting just a few hours, the Bolsheviks seize power from the Provisional Government. In the Soviet Union this putsch is known as the Great October Revolution. Russia's use of the old-style calendar until 1918 trailed the modern calendar by eleven days.

NOVEMBER The Moscow Soviet cuts Moscow rents by 50 per cent, and the following month it takes over all private housing in the city.

1918

3 MARCH Soviet Russia signs a peace treaty in Brest-Litovsk. It gives independence to the Baltic principalities,

Ukraine and parts of Poland, hands over more territory to the Ottomans, and binds Lenin's government to paying massive war reparations.

5 MARCH Moscow, by 1918 a city of somewhat less than 2 million people, is designated the capital of the Soviet Union, restoring it to the role it had lost when Peter the Great moved his government to St Petersburg 200 years earlier. The Communists take the decision partly for strategic reasons: the peace treaties struck with Germany lost Russia its Baltic and Polish provinces leaving what by then was called Petrograd dangerously exposed to a hostile border. But there are also symbolic reasons to turn their backs on a city associated with imperial power and create a socialist alternative.

12 APRIL Lenin publishes a government decree: *On the Removal of Monuments Raised in Honour of the Tsars and Their Servants and the Working out of Designs for Monuments to the Russian Socialist Revolution.* The idea for this decree came from Maxim Gorky, who himself had been inspired by the Italian friar Tommaso Campanella and his influential book *The City of the Sun* (1602). This work described a utopia based on equality and sexual freedom, in which manual labour was honoured. It presented a city that was decorated in such a way as to spell out these guiding principles. The Soviet Revolution, Gorky persuaded Lenin, could make its mark on Moscow in a similar way. Following the decree, Alexander II's statue in the Kremlin, and that of Alexander III in front of the

Cathedral of Christ the Saviour are both destroyed. Imperial insignia is chiselled off the Romanov memorial in the Aleksandrovsky gardens, to make way for a bust of Robespierre.

Lenin personally takes part in tearing down the memorial to Grand Duke Sergey Alexandrovich who, when governor of Moscow, had expelled 20,000 Jews from the city. Sergey Alexandrovich was also held partly responsible for the tragic deaths of over 1,000 people in a stampede at the celebrations for the coronation of Tsar Nicholas II. In 2016, President Putin would agree to a proposal to consider ways of rebuilding the lost monument.

Under the terms of Lenin's decree a commission is established to produce a list of some sixty individuals ranging from Spartacus to Darwin, who would be monumentalized around Moscow.

MAY The Moscow Soviet sets up a food committee and expels all students, ex-soldiers, refugees, 'parasites' and persons without defined occupations. They are given three weeks in which to leave the city, after which they would have no ration cards.

30 AUGUST A Russian Revolutionary named Fanny Kaplan fires three shots at Lenin as he leaves a factory in Moscow, badly injuring him. The appropriation and redistribution of housing in Moscow accelerates in the wake of this failed assassination attempt.

'The moment we got word of the wounding of Comrade Lenin by the Whites,

the commission declared Red Terror against the bourgeoisie and set about evicting them [...]. Workers moved into these large houses slowly at first because of the fuel shortage. After our commission sent a detachment of Communists into 31 Bolshaya Basmanaya, several thousand workers came over and occupied all the houses. This is how we solved the housing crisis' — Yakov Bazanov, chairman of the Basmannyi special housing commission.

1919

Lenin becomes the first living Communist to get a street named after him. On his death five years later, the city of Petrograd is renamed after him, a designation it carries until 1991 when the citizens of St Petersburg voted for yet another change.

1920

The VKhUTEMAS (the Higher Art and Technical Studios) is established from a merger of the first free arts studio, once the Stroganov College of Industrial Arts, and the second studio, once the Moscow College of Painting, Sculpture and Architecture.

1922

Stalin becomes general secretary of the Central Committee of the Communist Party of the Soviet Union.

1923 - 5

Moscow's city government considers a wide range of proposals for the reconstruction of the capital of the Soviet Union. The ideas of Ebenezer Howard and the English Garden City movement find some favour for a decentralized post-capitalist city. At the same time there is a drive toward communal living, and more radical explorations of new architectural forms, such as El Lissitzky's 'Cloud Iron' projects which proposed transforming the identity of Moscow with a ring of so-called horizontal skyscrapers.

1924

21 JANUARY Lenin dies after a long period of the illness brought on by a stroke that has weakened his effectiveness in resisting the accumulation of power by Stalin. The leader of the Communist revolution becomes the figure of a carefully constructed cult that takes on overt religious significance.

He is buried three times. In the first ceremony six days after his death, his body, contained in a refrigerated glass coffin, is placed in a small wooden crypt put together overnight by carpenters to a design by Alexey Shchusev. Moscow Radio calls on the whole Soviet Union to stand up at the moment of the interment, while 500,000 workers take part in a six-hour-long march past the grave itself.

1931

JULY Demolition of the Cathedral of Christ the Saviour starts. Molotov chairs the building council. It takes dynamite and five months' labour to shift the 18 million bricks that went into its foundations. Stalin's men also saw to the destruction of 11 of Moscow's 25 monasteries. One of them became a car park for government limousines.

1932

MARCH Building of Moscow's metro system gets underway.

1932-3

Soviet Famine; Stalin's agricultural collectivization policies trigger a catastrophic famine across the USSR which causes millions of deaths. Work starts on building the 416-metre-high Palace of the Soviets, and its 100-metre-high statue of Lenin.

1937

Start of the great purges.

1939

Hitler-Stalin pact of non-aggression signed.

1941

Hitler invades the Soviet Union. Work is halted on the Palace of the Soviets, with steelwork having reached the eleventh floor.

1947

1 JANUARY Stalin announces a plan to build eight socialist classical-style skyscrapers. The seven that were completed by 1952, with the use of forced labour, still define Moscow's skyline (the eighth was never built).

1953

5 MARCH Stalin dies.

1956

Khruschchev delivers his speech 'On the Cult of Personality and its Consequences' in a secret session of the Soviet Communist Party, denouncing Stalin's deviation from Leninist principles. The architecture of Stalinism is specifically mentioned, and Khruschchev goes on to promote a more 'scientific' functionalism.

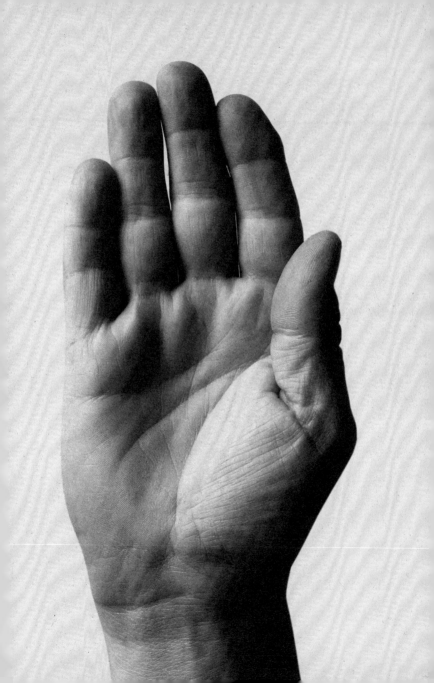

BIOGRAPHIES

RICHARD ANDERSON

Richard Anderson is Lecturer in Architectural History at the University of Edinburgh. He specializes in the history of modern and contemporary architecture in North America, Europe and Eurasia. His essays have appeared in *AA Files*, *Grey Room*, *Log* and *Future Anterior*, among other journals and edited volumes. He is editor and principal translator of Ludwig Hilberseimer's *Metropolisarchitecture* and *Selected Essays* (2012) and the author of *Russia: Modern Architectures in History* (2015), a cultural history of Russian architecture from 1861 to the present. His current research explores the global effects of the Soviet architectural system.

JEAN-LOUIS COHEN

Trained as an architect and historian, Jean-Louis Cohen has been Chair for the History of Architecture at New York University's Institute of Fine Arts since 1994. Since 2014, he has been a guest professor at the Collège de France. His forty books include *Architecture in Uniform* (2011), *The Future of Architecture Since 1889* (2012), and *Le Corbusier: An Atlas of Modern Landscapes* (2013). He has curated numerous exhibitions, including *Scenes of the World to Come* at the Canadian Centre for Architecture (1995), *Interférences / Interferenzen — Architecture, Allemagne, France* at the Musées de Strasbourg (2013), and *L'Aventure Le Corbusier* at the Centre Pompidou (1987).

ESZTER STEIERHOFFER

Eszter Steierhoffer is Curator at the Design Museum in London. Previously she worked as Curator of Contemporary Architecture at the Canadian Centre for Architecture in Montreal. She holds a PhD from the Royal College of Art in Critical and Historical Studies and her research interests include the history of modern and contemporary architecture exhibitions. She has organized numerous exhibitions and symposia with architectural foci, including *Corner, Block, Neighbourhood, Cities. Álvaro Siza in Berlin and The Hague* (2015); *Zoo-topia. On zoo architecture as taxonomies of national representation* (2012); and *Anatomy of a Street* (2010).

DEYAN SUDJIC

Deyan Sudjic is Director of the Design Museum. His career has spanned journalism, teaching and writing. He was the editor of Domus magazine from 2000 to 2004, and founding editor of *Blueprint* magazine. He has published many books on design and architecture, including *The Edifice Complex* (2005), *The Language of Things* (2008), *Norman Foster: A Life in Architecture* (2010), *Shiro Kuramata* (2013) and *B is for Bauhaus* (2015). His most recent book, *Ettore Sottsass and the Poetry of Things*, was published by Phaidon in September 2015.

PICTURE CREDITS

Gustav Klutsis,
Photomontage,
lithography on paper,
17 × 25.7, 1924,
Ne boltai! Collection
(Cover image)

INTRODUCTION: IMAGINE MOSCOW

Arkady Shaikhet,
Steelworks, vintage
gelatin silver print,
29.3 × 40, 1935,
Alex Lachmann
Collection
(6)

El Lissitzky, *Plan of
the Centre of Moscow
with Skyscrapers
in Ring A*, 1923-5,
printed in
*ASNOVA:
The Association of
New Architects*, 1926
(8)

Unknown,
VKhUTEMAS
architecture students
with three-dimen-
sional models,
black and white
photography, 1920s
(9)

Ilya Chashnik,
Suprematist Ornament,
mixed media on
paper, 28.8 × 22.3,
1927-8, Sepherot
Foundation
(10)

Boris Iofan,
Vladimir Gelfreikh
and Vladimir
Shchuko, *The Palace
of the Soviets*, model,
black and white
photography,
9 × 12, 1937, Shchusev
State Museum of
Architecture
(12)

Scene from the 1933
film *King Kong*,
AP Photo
(12)

Kuehn Malvezzi
Architects, *Imagine
Moscow: Architecture,
Propaganda, Revolution*,
exhibition plan, 2017
(14)

CLOUD IRON: COLONIZING THE SKY

El Lissitzky, *Design for
the Cloud Iron*, views
from the Kremlin,
photograph with
architect's annotations,
12.6 × 16.9, 1925,
Collection Van
Abbemuseum,
Eindhoven
(21)

El Lissitzky, *Proun 1E
(The City)*, lithograph
on paper, 28.6 × 24.1,
1919-21, Private
Collection, Moscow
(22)

Yakov Chernikhov, *101
Architectural Fantasies,
composition no. 57*,
gouache on paper,
24 × 30, 1933,
Alex Lachmann
Collection
(23)

Gustav Klutsis,
Architectural Study,
mixed media on paper,
24.8 × 39.5, 1921-2,
Annely Juda Fine Art,
London
(24)

Innokenty Kychakov,
*Festival Design, Central
Park for Culture and
Recovery (Gorky Park)*,
mixed media on paper,
52.3 × 30.7, 1929,
Alex Lachmann
Collection
(25)

El Lissitzky, *Proun*,
mixed media on
paper, 50 × 52, 1922-3,
Collection Van
Abbemuseum,
Eindhoven
(26)

Lyubov Popova,
*Suprematist
Composition*,
collage on paper,
24.3 × 32.5, 1917,
Sepherot Foundation
(27)

Ilya Chashnik,
*Project for a Suprematist
Monument*, mixed
media on paper,
28.8 × 22.3, 1927,
Sepherot Foundation
(28)

Ilya Chashnik,
Red Square UNOVIS,
mixed media on paper,
19.4 × 21.4, 1924,
Private Collection,
Moscow
(29)

Nikolai Suetin,
Sketch for a Chair,
mixed media on paper,
14.9 × 23.5, 1927,
Sepherot Foundation
(30)

Nikolai Suetin,
*Suprematist Surface
Forms*, textile design,
ink on paper,
32.5 × 23.5, c 1921,
Private Collection,
Moscow
(31)

Sergey Burylin for
Ivanovo-Voznesensk
Factories, 'Airplane',
textile fragment,
13.8 × 8, 1929,
The Lloyd Cotsen
Textile Traces
Study Collection
(32)

Pesochenskaya
Pottery Factory,
'And our ultimatum',
ceramic, 24.3 (d), 1929,
Collection of Vladimir
Tsarenkov, London
(33)

Valentina Kulagina,
'To the defence of
the USSR', poster,
72.4 × 90.9, 1931,
Ne boltai! Collection
(34)

Maria Bri-Bein,
'Woman proletarian,
seize aircraft,
go to schools and
colleges of civil
aviation!', poster,
71.5 × 101.5, 1931,
Ne boltai! Collection
(35)

LENIN INSTITUTE: EDUCATING THE NEW MAN

Ivan Leonidov,
Lenin Institute,
printed in *Contemporary Architecture*,
no. 4-5, 1927
(39)

Ivan Leonidov,
*United Nations
Building*, mixed
media on paper,
20 × 17.7, 1947-8,
© Tchoban
Foundation
(40)

Ivan Leonidov,
The *City of the Sun,
Distant View*, mixed
media on paper,
15.2 × 40, 1943-59,
© Tchoban
Foundation
(41)

Ivan Leonidov,
The City of the Sun,
mixed media on paper,
48.3 × 33.5, 1957-8,
Alex Lachmann
Collection
(42)

Ivan Leonidov,
*Monument to the
First Sputnik*, paint
on wood panel,
27.5 × 23.5, 1958,
Alex Lachmann
Collection
(43)

Nikolay Kogout,
'From darkness to
light, from battle
to book, from
misery to happiness',
poster, 70 × 52, 1921,
Ne boltai! Collection
(44)

Unknown,
'Worldwide Peoples'
Armed Forces', poster,
49.1 × 58.6, 1919,
Ne boltai! Collection
(45)

Designed for
Trekhgornaya
Manufacturing,
textile design,
watercolour on paper,
35.9 × 27.6, c 1920,
The Lloyd Cotsen
Textile Traces Study
Collection
(46)

Karel Teige,
1917-1927,
postcard, 1927,
Ne boltai! Collection
(47)

Boris Efimov,
*Our Rise ... And Their
Landing*, print on
paper, 15×24, 1933,
Ne boltai! Collection
(48)

Alexander Rodchenko, *Circus-Acrobats*,
vintage gelatin silver
print, 23 × 29.3, 1938,
Alex Lachmann
Collection
(49)

HEALTH FACTORY: THE BODY AS MACHINE

Nikolay Sokolov
Hotel Resort, Individual House, mixed media
on paper,
36.2 × 108.5, 1928,
Shchusev State
Museum of
Architecture
(53)

Nikolay Sokolov
*Hotel Resort, Individual
House*, mixed media
on paper,
69.8 × 50.2, 1928,
Shchusev State
Museum of
Architecture
(54)

Nikolay Sokolov, *Hotel
Resort, Social Complex*,
mixed media on paper,
88.2 × 55.5, 1928,
Shchusev State
Museum of
Architecture
(55)

El Lissitzky, design
for magazine cover,
linocut on paper,
19.8 × 27, 1922,
Collection Van
Abbemuseum,
Eindhoven
(56)

Platon Ippolitov,
'Free aerobics',
postcard, 1933,
Ne boltai! Collection
(57)

El Lissitzky, three-dimensional design
for the electro-mechanical opera,
*Victory Over the Sun,
The New Man*,
lithograph on paper,
45.5 × 53, 1923,
Collection Van
Abbemuseum,
Eindhoven
(58)

Rajnis, *Untitled*,
postcard, 1926,
Ne boltai! Collection
(59)

Ivanovo-Voznesensk
Factories,
textile fragment,
18.7 × 15.9, 1928-32,
The Lloyd Cotsen
Textile Traces Study
Collection
(60)

Vera Gitsevich,
*For the Proletarian Park
of Culture and Leisure*,
photocollage, gouache
on photo paper,
12.7 × 18.4, 1930s,
Ne boltai! Collection
(61)

COMMUNAL HOUSE: EMANCIPATING WOMEN

Nikolay Ladovsky,
Communal House,
pencil on paper,
31.5 × 39, 1919,
Shchusev State
Museum of
Architecture
(65)

Georgy Mapu,
Communal House,
pencil on paper,
12 × 18, 1919-20,
Alex Lachmann
Collection
(66)

Georgy Mapu
Communal House,
floor plan, mixed
media on paper,
27 × 36, 1920,
Alex Lachmann
Collection
(67)

Georgy Mapu,
Communal House,
pencil on paper,
20.5 × 25.5, 1919-20,
Alex Lachmann
Collection
(68)

Elizaveta Nikitina
for the First Factory
of Printed Cotton,
'Children playing',
textile fragment,
12 × 14.4, 1928-30,
The Lloyd Cotsen
Textile Traces
Study Collection
(69)

Oskar Arjun for
Trekhgornaya
Manufacturing,
textile fragment,
10.6 × 11.4, 1928-32,
The Lloyd Cotsen
Textile Traces
Study Collection
(70)

Vera Latonina,
'The end of illiteracy',
textile fragment,
12.7 × 12.4, 1928-33,
The Lloyd Cotsen
Textile Traces
Study Collection
(71)

Unknown,
'By organizing
day nurseries,
playgrounds, kitchen
factories, canteens
and mechanical
laundries, we will
get 1,600,000 new
working women',
poster, 52.7 × 71.7, 1931,
Ne boltai! Collection
(72)

Valentina Kulagina,
*The international
Day of Working
Women*, poster,
71.5 × 109, 1930,
Ne boltai! Collection
(73)

Unknown,
'We create exemplary
institutions, canteens,
nurseries', poster,
35.5 × 28, 1930s,
Ne boltai! Collection
(74)

Valentina Kulagina,
Krasnaya Niva N. 12,
magazine,
23 × 30, 1930,
Ne boltai! Collection
(75)

COMMISSARIAT OF HEAVY INDUSTRY: INDUSTRY IS THE NEW LANDSCAPE

Vesnin Brothers,
Commissariat of
Heavy Industry
competition entry,
mixed media
on paper,
196.6 × 138.5, 1934,
Shchusev State
Museum of
Architecture
(79)

Ivan Leonidov,
Commissariat of
Heavy Industry
competition entry,
mixed media
on paper,
117.5 × 182.2, 1934,
Shchusev State
Museum of
Architecture
(80)

Konstantin Melnikov,
Commissariat of
Heavy Industry
competition entry,
mixed media
on paper,
150.1 × 148.3, 1934,
Shchusev State
Museum of
Architecture
(81)

Yakov Chernikhov,
Architectural Fairytale,
mixed media on
paper, 24 × 30, 1933,
© Tchoban
Foundation
(82)

Gustav Klutsis,
Lenin in a Factory,
photomontage,
12 × 8.5, c 1929,
Ne boltai! Collection
(83)

Arkady Shaikhet,
*Assembling at a
Metal Plant*, vintage
gelatin silver print,
18 × 23.9, 1930s,
Alex Lachmann
Collection
(84)

Yakov Chernikhov,
Architectural Fairytale,
mixed media on
paper, 24 × 30,
late 1920s,
© Tchoban
Foundation
(85)

Valentina Kulagina,
'We build',
postcard, c 1930,
Ne boltai! Collection
(86)

Yakov Chernikhov,
Untitled, ink on paper,
12 × 12, 1920, Drawing
Matter Collections
(87)

Designed for Trekhgornaya Manufacturing, textile design, watercolour on paper, 20.9 × 21.6, c 1930, The Lloyd Cotsen Textile Traces Study Collection (88)

Gustav Klutsis, *Untitled*, photomontage, 11.5 × 24.7, 1930, Ne boltai! Collection (89)

PALACE OF THE SOVIETS: THE ETERNAL MONUMENT

Boris Iofan, Vladimir Gelfreikh and Vladimir Shchuko, *The Palace of the Soviets*, mixed media on paper, c 1937 (93)

Unknown, 'Historical development of the skyline of central Moscow', reproduction, 18 × 24, undated, Shchusev State Museum of Architecture (94-5)

Boris Iofan, *The Palace of the Soviets*, view of the interior, mixed media on paper, 41.3 × 55, 1944, © Tchoban Foundation (96)

Boris Iofan, Vladimir Gelfreikh and Vladimir Shchuko, *The Palace of the Soviets, Final Version*, mixed media on paper, 193.5 × 129, 1937, Shchusev State Museum of Architecture (97)

Boris Iofan, *The Palace of the Soviets*, pencil on paper, 64 × 50, c 1933, Alex Lachmann Collection (98)

Boris Iofan, *The Palace of the Soviets*, pencil on paper, 53 × 43, 1933-7, Alex Lachmann Collection (99)

Boris Iofan, *The Palace of the Soviets*, pencil, charcoal on paper, 53 × 43, c 1933, Alex Lachmann Collection (100)

Gustav Klutsis, *Untitled*, photomontage, 9.3 × 13.2, 1929 Ne boltai! Collection (101)

Gustav Klutsis, *Untitled*, photomontage, 88.4 × 122.3, 1930, Ne boltai! Collection (102)

LENIN MAUSOLEUM: CULT OF THE LEADER

Alexey Shchusev, *Lenin Mausoleum*, watercolour on paper, 54 × 45, 1924, Alex Lachmann Collection (107)

Gustav Klutsis, *Monument to our Fallen Leaders*, maquette, 58.8 × 38.5, 1924, Ne boltai! Collection (108)

Gustav Klutsis, *Monument to our Fallen Leaders*, maquette, 58.8 × 38.5, 1924, Ne boltai! Collection (109)

Unknown, 'Lenin's city is the city of universal literacy', poster, 69.5 × 102, 1931, Ne boltai! Collection (111)

Georgy Kibardin, 'We will build Lenin's squadron of airships', poster, 72.6 × 104, 1931, Ne boltai! Collection (112)

Mikhail Balyasny 'We will make the USSR the country of socialist industry and electrification', poster, 70.3 × 99.7, 1930, Ne boltai! Collection (113)

P Ustinov, Competition entry for the Lenin Mausoleum in Moscow, mixed media on paper, 1924, © RGASPI (114)

P Korolev and S Maklashev, Competition entry for the Lenin Mausoleum in Moscow, 1924, © RGASPI (115)

B Prokhorov, *Competition entry for the Lenin Mausoleum in Moscow*, 1924, © RGASPI (116)

A Smirnov, Competition entry for the Lenin Mausoleum in Moscow, mixed media on paper, 1924, © RGASPI (116)

N Ryabov, Competition entry for the Lenin Mausoleum in Moscow, mixed media on paper, 1924, © RGASPI (117)

P Berkutov, Competition entry for the Lenin Mausoleum in Moscow, mixed media on paper, 1924, © RGASPI (118)

THE SPECTACLE OF SOCIALIST MOSCOW

John Heartfield, *Montage of Lenin over Moscow*, black and white photograph, 1931, Artists Rights Society (ARS), New York / VG Bild-Kunst, Bonn
(122)

Aleksandr Vesnin and Lyubov Popova, *Spectacle for the Third International*, Moscow, 1921, Khan-Magomedov, S. O.
(123)

Model of Ivan Leonidov's 'Lenin Institute of Library Sciences', First Exhibition of Modern Architecture, Moscow, 1927, *Sovremennaia arkhitektura*, nos. 4-5
(125)

Mikhail Barshch and Viacheslav Vladimirov, *Experimental Design for a Communal House*, 1929, *Sovremennaia arkhitektura*, no. 4
(126)

Lev Rudnev's project for the Red Army Theatre, Architectural Exhibition on Gorky Street, Moscow, 1933, *Arkhitektura SSSR*, no. 1
(128)

Panorama of Moscow developed according to the 1935 Plan, 1936, *Moskovskii rabochii*
(129)

LISSITZKY'S 'AMERIKANIZM'

El Lissitzky, *Design for the Cloud Iron in Moscow*, view from Strastnoy Boulevard, photograph with architect's annotations, 13.5 × 13, 1925, Collection Van Abbemuseum, Eindhoven
(131)

El Lissitzky, *Design for the Cloud Iron in Moscow*, aerial view, photograph with architect's annotations, 13.5 × 13, 1925, Collection Van Abbemuseum, Eindhoven
(132)

THE SOCIALIST VATICAN

Photo of the destruction of the original Church of Christ the Saviour in Moscow, Russia, 1931
(140)

Boris Iofan, *The Palace of the Soviets*, pencil on paper, 43 × 54, 1933-7, Alex Lachmann Collection
(141)

Boris Iofan, *Iofan's workshop in drawing the project of the Palace of the Soviets*, 1930s, Shchusev State Museum of Architecture
(141)

Boris Iofan, *Iofan's perspective of the 416-metre Palace of Soviets*, 1937
(142)

N Granovsky, Open-air swimming pool 'Moscow', photographic film, black and white negative, 6 × 9, c 1960, Shchusev State Museum of Architecture
(144)

Phil Sayer, the Leningradskaya Hotel, Moscow, one of the seven Stalin towers, 2001, © Phil Sayer
(145)

TEXT CREDIT

El Lissitzky, '"Americanism" in European Architecture', in *El Lissitzky: Life, Letters, Text*, trans. Sophie Lissitzky-Küppers (London: Thames and Hudson, 1980), 373-5.

Original German text and English translation © Philo Fine Arts Stiftung & Co.KG, Hamburg/Germany, 1967
(134-8)

EXHIBITION ACKNOWLEDGEMENTS

This book was published in conjunction with
the exhibition *Imagine Moscow: Architecture,
Propaganda, Revolution* at the Design Museum,
London, 15 March 2017 to 4 June 2017.

Curator: Eszter Steierhoffer
Curatorial Assistant: Eleanor Watson
Curatorial Research Assistants: Kristina Ailane,
Helen Ikla, Constanza Larach, Anya Smirnova
and Olga Vaigatcheva
Exhibition Project Managers: Rebecca England
and Miranda Stacey
Exhibitions Coordinator: Emily Durant
Senior Technician: Stuart Robertson
Exhibition Design: Kuehn Malvezzi, Berlin
Exhibition Graphic Design: Kellenberger-White

Special thanks go to colleagues and friends
who have generously shared their knowledge
and precious advice to aid the curatorial
development of the exhibition: Yuri Avvakumov,
Anna Bronovitskaya, Clem Cecil, Jean-Louis Cohen,
David Crowley, Péter György, Justin McGuirk,
Mark Nash, Daria Nuzhnaya, Ekaterina Savina,
Nikolai Vassiliev and Gergely Kovács, as well as
Galina Andreeva and Alexandra Savenkova from
the All Russian Applied Arts Museum in Moscow;
Tatiana Ilyina and Evgenia Gerasimova from the
British Council Russia; Mel Bach from the
Catherine Cooke Collection in Cambridge;
Alexandra Selivanova from the Museum of
Moscow; Anna Loginova from the Ne boltai!
Collection in Prague; Maria Kostyuk,
Maria Rogozina and Elena Zheludkova from
the Shchushev State Museum of Architecture in
Moscow; Katerina Chuchalina and Anna Ilchenko
from V-A-C Foundation in Moscow.

The Design Museum owes its gratitude to the
lenders of the exhibition: Alex Lachmann
Collection, Annely Juda Fine Art, Architectural
Association, British Pathe, Catherine Cooke
Collection, Drawing Matter, James Butterwick,
Net-Film, RGASPI, The Cotsen Collection,
Ne boltai! Foundation, Sepherot Foundation,
Shchusev State Museum of Architecture,
Tchoban Foundation, Vladimir Tsarenkov,
and the Van Abbemuseum.

BOOK ACKNOWLEDGEMENTS

Thanks to Jean-Louis Cohen for his invaluable advice and contribution, to John English, Jessica Read, Jasper Fry and Jason Elphick from Pureprint Group, and to the designers of this catalogue, Stina Gromark and Louise N Morgan of Stinsensqueeze.

Many colleagues at the Design Museum have contributed to this book, and thanks go to them all.

the Design Museum
224-238 Kensington High Street
London W8 6AG

designmuseum.org

First published in 2017
© 2017 the Design Museum

ISBN 978 1 8720 0536 2

Publishing Manager: Mark Cortes Favis
Publishing Coordinator: Ianthe Fry
Picture Researcher: Anabel Navarro Llorens
Editorial Assistants: Eleanor Watson and Olga Vaigatcheva

Designers: Stinsensqueeze

Printed in the UK